REVISE EDEXCEL GCSE (9–1)

D1152230

History

EARLY ELIZABETHAN ENGLAND, 1558–88

REVISION
GUIDE AND WORKBOOK

Series Consultant: Harry Smith

Author: Brian Dowse

A note from the publisher

In order to ensure that this resource offers high-quality support for the associated Pearson qualification, it has been through a review process by the awarding body. This process confirms that this resource fully covers the teaching and learning content of the specification or part of a specification at which it is aimed. It also confirms that it demonstrates an appropriate balance between the development of subject skills, knowledge and understanding, in addition to preparation for assessment.

Endorsement does not cover any guidance on assessment activities or processes (e.g. practice questions or advice on how to answer assessment questions), included in the resource nor does it prescribe any particular approach to the teaching or delivery of a related course.

While the publishers have made every attempt to ensure that advice on the qualification and its assessment is accurate, the official specification and associated assessment guidance materials are the only authoritative source of information and should always be referred to for definitive guidance.

Pearson examiners have not contributed to any sections in this resource relevant to examination papers for which they have responsibility.

Examiners will not use endorsed resources as a source of material for any assessment set by Pearson.

Endorsement of a resource does not mean that the resource is required to achieve this Pearson qualification, nor does it mean that it is the only suitable material available to support the qualification, and any resource lists produced by the awarding body shall include this and other appropriate resources.

For the full range of Pearson revision titles across KS2, KS3, GCSE, Functional Skills, AS/A Level and BTEC visit:
www.pearsonschools.co.uk/revise

Contents

. . . .

A small bit of small print

Edexcel publishes Sample Assessment Material and the Specification on its website. This is the official content and this book should be used in conjunction with it. The questions in *Now try this* have been written to help you practise every topic in the book. Remember: the real exam questions may not look like this.

Government on Elizabeth's accession

Elizabethan government had many different features and involved the court, the Privy Council, parliament, Lord Lieutenants and Justices of the Peace.

Elizabeth's government

The court – made up of noblemen who acted as the monarch's advisers and friends. They advised the monarch and helped display her wealth and power. Members of the court could also be members of the Privy Council.

The Privy Council – members of the nobility who helped govern the country. They monitored parliament, Justices of the Peace and oversaw law and order and the security of the country.

Elizabeth I became queen of England in 1558.

Parliament – advised Elizabeth's government, made up of the House of Lords and the House of Commons.
The House of Lords was made up of noblemen and bishops.
The House of Commons was elected, though very few people could vote.
Parliament passed laws and approved taxes (**extraordinary taxation**).

Justices of the Peace – large landowners; appointed by government, who kept law and order locally and heard court cases.

Lord Lieutenants – noblemen, appointed by government, who governed English counties and raised the local **militia**.

Key terms

Extraordinary taxation – extra taxes required to pay for unexpected expenses, especially war.

Militia – a force of ordinary people (not professional soldiers) raised in an emergency.

Remember: Elizabeth did not possess complete power. She could not pass laws without parliament's approval, or raise taxes without parliament's agreement.

Now try this

1 Explain **two** features of Elizabethan government.
2 Were there any ways in which the power of Queen Elizabeth I was limited? Explain your answer.

 You may wish to refer to parliament when answering this question.

Society on Elizabeth's accession

Elizabethan society was very rigid, based on inequality and a social hierarchy or structure where everyone knew their place.

The social hierarchy of the countryside

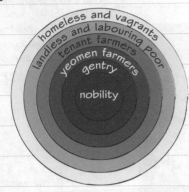

90% of the population of Elizabethan England lived in the countryside.

The social hierarchy of towns

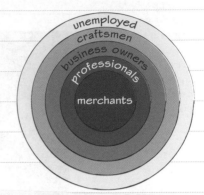

10% of the population of Elizabethan England lived in towns.

Who's who in the countryside

- ✓ **The nobility** – major landowners; often lords, dukes and earls.
- ✓ **The gentry** – owned smaller estates.
- ✓ **The yeoman farmers** – owned a small amount of land.
- ✓ **Tenant farmers** – rented land from the yeoman farmers and gentry.
- ✓ **The landless and labouring poor** – people who did not own or rent land, and had to work or labour to provide for themselves and their families.
- ✓ **Homeless and vagrants** – moved from place to place looking for work.

Who's who in the towns

- ✓ **Merchants** – traders who were very wealthy.
- ✓ **Professionals** – lawyers, doctors and clergymen.
- ✓ **Business owners** – often highly skilled craftsmen, such as silversmiths, glovers (glove makers), carpenters or tailors.
- ✓ **Craftsmen** – skilled employees, including apprentices.
- ✓ **Unskilled labourers and the unemployed** – people who had no regular work and could not provide for themselves and their families.

Obedience and care

Wherever you were in Elizabethan society, you owed respect and obedience to those above you and had a duty of care to those below. Landowners ran their estates according to these ideas. Ideally they would take care of their tenants, especially during times of hardship.

Households were run along similar lines to society. The husband and father was head of the household. His wife, children and any servants were expected to be obedient to him.

Now try this

Briefly explain **two** features of Elizabethan society.

A **feature** is an aspect of a topic. For example, obedience and care is a feature of Elizabethan society.

Virgin Queen: legitimacy, gender and marriage

When Elizabeth became queen following the death of her older sister, Mary, she had to find a way of establishing her authority as reigning monarch.

Elizabeth was young (21 years old) and lacked experience.

Elizabeth's government needed money.

Elizabeth's **legitimacy** was in doubt as the pope had refused to recognise her mother's marriage to Henry VIII.

Problems facing Elizabeth when she became queen

To pass laws, Elizabeth needed the support of parliament.

Catholics refused to acknowledge Elizabeth's right to rule England.

Elizabeth was unmarried and it was unusual for a queen to rule in her own right, as Christian traditions suggested that women should follow men's authority. Many people disapproved of the idea of a queen regnant (a queen who actually ruled).

Elizabeth was Protestant. Her predecessor, Mary, was Catholic.

Elizabeth's father, Henry VIII, had divorced Catherine of Aragon and married Anne Boleyn, Elizabeth's mother. The pope refused to recognise this divorce. When Anne Boleyn was executed in 1536, Henry excluded Elizabeth from the succession, although he reversed this decision before his death.

Legitimacy refers to whether a monarch is lawfully entitled to rule.

Many Catholics, especially in the north, disliked the way Henry had taken over the Church in 1534 (the Act of Supremacy) and dissolved the monasteries. They questioned Elizabeth's legitimacy, claiming that she had no right to rule. They preferred a Catholic monarch and there was a real risk of rebellion.

Key issues facing Elizabeth in 1588

- It was widely expected that Elizabeth would marry. However, this would reduce Elizabeth's power, as her husband would be expected to govern the country and deal with parliament.

- Elizabeth's inexperience meant that she needed the support and advice of her Privy Council, especially her Secretary of State, Sir William Cecil.

- Elizabeth could issue royal proclamations and had prerogative powers, enabling her to govern without parliament's consent, especially in foreign policy. However, laws could only be passed with parliament's approval as Acts of Parliament.

The problems of marriage

- ✓ If Elizabeth married a Protestant, this would anger Catholics.
- ✓ If she married a Catholic, this would upset Protestants.
- ✓ Marriage could involve England in expensive wars, damaging royal finances and requiring taxation. The Crown was already £300 000 in debt.

Yet marriage was important, as Elizabeth needed an heir. If she died without an heir the throne would be vacant and this could lead to civil war.

> ### Now try this
>
> Briefly explain **two** problems Elizabeth faced when she became queen in 1558.

Virgin Queen: character and strengths

Elizabeth was known as 'the Virgin Queen' because she remained unmarried. Many people in the 16th century felt this meant she could not rule alone. However, Elizabeth had a number of strengths as a ruling monarch.

Elizabeth's character and strengths

Elizabeth was confident and **charismatic** – this enabled her to win over her subjects and command support in parliament.

Elizabeth was resilient – she had spent time in the Tower accused of treason and facing possible execution. She could cope with the pressures of being queen.

The Virgin Queen

Elizabeth was well educated – she spoke Latin, Greek, French and Italian.

Elizabeth had an excellent grasp of politics – she understood the interests and ambitions of her subjects, and was able to use her powers of **patronage** effectively.

Although Elizabeth was **Protestant**, the number of Protestants in England was growing, making her position as queen more secure. She could claim **divine right** with growing conviction.

Reinventing the role

Elizabeth was able to use her strengths to reinvent herself as a different type of monarch. She liked to demonstrate that, even though she was female, she was no ordinary woman. She therefore argued that she did not need to marry and could govern England on her own.

Elizabethan propaganda

Throughout her reign, Elizabeth was happy to portray herself as a strong, legitimate, popular monarch and a 'Virgin Queen' – married only to England and not to a prince or king. This is reflected in paintings such as the one above of her coronation, which shows a confident but feminine monarch rightfully crowned queen.

Key terms

- **Charismatic leader** – someone who possesses great personal appeal and can use this to win people over.
- **Legitimate ruler** – someone who is legally and morally entitled to rule.
- **Divine right** – the idea that God alone appointed the monarch, meaning that to challenge the monarch was to challenge God. Successful monarchs claimed divine providence (Godly approval) of their actions, reinforcing their legitimacy. Less successful monarchs could face charges of Godly disapproval and find their legitimacy undermined.
- **Protestants** – Christians who no longer accepted the authority of the pope and many of the teachings of the Roman Catholic Church. During the Reformation (which began in 1517), Protestants, under Martin Luther, seceded (broke away from) the Roman Catholic Church, and this resulted in religious wars in France and Germany.
- **Patronage** – the monarch could use the granting of lands, jobs and titles to reward her supporters. People who received these positions could use them to become wealthy.

Now try this

Briefly describe **two** advantages Elizabeth had when she became queen in 1558.

Challenges at home: financial weaknesses

Elizabeth faced a number of financial challenges at home when she became queen.

Financial weaknesses in 1558

There was a need to improve the quality of money to help England's finances.

- The **Crown** was £300 000 in debt and had an annual income of only £286 667.

- Over £100 000 of Crown debts was owed to foreign moneylenders (the Antwerp Exchange), which charged a high interest rate at 14%.

- Mary Tudor had sold off Crown lands to pay for wars with France, so the Crown's income from rents was falling.

- Elizabeth needed money to remain secure on the throne, as she could use it to reward her supporters.

- Since the 1540s, the Crown had debased (devalued) the coinage, by reducing its silver and gold content, in order to make more money to fight wars against France. This resulted in **inflation**, as the value of the currency fell.

The word **Crown** refers to the government, which means the monarch and her advisers (Privy Councillors).

How monarchs could raise money

- Rents and income from their own lands (Crown lands).
- Taxes from trade (known as customs duties).
- Special additional taxes, known as subsidies, which had to be agreed by parliament.
- Profits of justice (fines, property or lands from people convicted of crimes).
- Loans (sometimes loans were 'forced', meaning they were compulsory and never repaid).

Inflation is where prices rise. This happened because coins were worth less, so people charged more for what they sold.

What could Elizabeth do to solve her financial problems in 1558?

Raise taxes to boost the Crown's income

👍 The queen could convene parliament and ask for subsidies (special additional taxes).

👎 Additional taxes would be unpopular with ordinary people, increasing the risk of unrest.

Improve the quality of money by increasing the gold and silver content in the coinage.

👍 In 1560, Thomas Gresham, the Crown's financial adviser, suggested this to William Cecil, but the Crown was slow to respond.

👎 Any 'new' coinage would be traded alongside older, less valuable coins. People would struggle to exchange the older coins for new ones.

The effects of Elizabeth's policies

In spite of Elizabeth's careful management of Crown finances, there was limited reform. Parliamentary grants were raised locally, with many landowners acting as Lord Lieutenants and Justices of the Peace, pocketing some of the proceeds before the rest was sent to the Crown. This meant that ordinary people faced a heavier financial burden while the wealthy benefitted.

What Elizabeth did

👍 She did not raise taxes but instead hoarded her income and cut her household expenses by half.

👍 Like her predecessors, she sold Crown lands, raising £120 000.

By 1574, the queen could claim that the Crown was out of debt for the first time since 1558.

Now try this

Explain why Elizabeth faced so many financial problems at the start of her reign in 1558.

Challenges abroad: France, Scotland and Spain

When she became queen in 1558, Elizabeth faced a number of challenges from France, Scotland and, to a lesser extent, Spain and its influence in the Netherlands.

Challenges from abroad facing Elizabeth in 1558

The French threat: France was wealthier than England and had a bigger population. Elizabeth's cousin, Mary, Queen of Scots, was married to the French king, Francis II. Mary had a strong claim to the English throne and English Catholics might rally to her if the French invaded.

Under the Treaty of Cateau-Cambrésis England had lost Calais to France. This was England's last remaining territory on the continent and there was pressure on Elizabeth to regain it. However, war with France would be expensive and dangerous.

The Auld Alliance: France's alliance with Scotland threatened England. Mary of Guise (James V's widow), who ruled Scotland on behalf of her daughter, Mary, Queen of Scots, kept French soldiers there, who could attack England. The relationship between France and Scotland was further strengthened by the marriage of Francis II (King of France) to Mary, Queen of Scots, in 1559.

Challenges abroad in 1588

France had ended its war with Spain. French military resources were no longer stretched by war with Spain, making a war with England more likely. There was also the possibility that France and Spain, both Catholic countries, would unite against Protestant England. Spain also had troops in the Netherlands, not far from England.

War was an expensive business and the Crown was in debt. England could not afford a war with France, Scotland or Spain, as this would be ruinously expensive and deepen the government's debts.

How Elizabeth dealt with the challenges from abroad

Elizabeth did her best to avoid upsetting Europe's most powerful countries.

- She sought to avoid war with France by signing the Peace of Troyes (1564), which recognised once and for all the French claim to Calais.
- Elizabeth was able to deal with the threat posed by Scotland by placing Mary, Queen of Scots, who fled Scotland in 1568, in custody in England.
- By imprisoning Mary and making peace with France, Elizabeth had only one significant threat by 1569: Spain.

Now try this

Explain the challenges Elizabeth faced abroad between 1558 and 1568.

Go to pages 13 and 14 to find out more about how Elizabeth dealt with the threat posed by Mary, Queen of Scots, between 1568 and 1569.

Religious divisions in England in 1558

Elizabeth was a Protestant queen taking over a country that was still largely Catholic.

Why was religion important in Elizabethan England?

- Religion was central to life in England. Religious teaching and practices guided people's morals and behaviour as well as their understanding of the world. Birth, marriage and death were all marked by religious ceremonies.
- People believed that going to church, attending pilgrimages and confessing sins reduced time in purgatory where the soul was purged of sin using 'spiritual fire' before reaching heaven.
- Religious festivals (holy days), such as St Swithin's Day (15 July) and Lammas Day (2 August), marked the agricultural year and were seen as essential to a good harvest.

Protestants tended to be found in northern Europe, especially in the Netherlands, Scandinavia and Germany.

The Reformation divided the Christian Church between Catholics and Protestants from 1517.

Religious divisions in England and Europe in the 16th century

Since the 1530s, many Protestants fleeing persecution in Europe had landed in England, settling in London, East Anglia and Kent. The number of English Protestants was growing.

The north of England, especially Durham, Yorkshire and Lancashire, remained largely Catholic.

Some Protestants became Puritans – people who wanted to purify the Christian religion by getting rid of anything not in the Bible.

The differences between Catholicism, Protestantism and Puritanism

	Catholics ('old religion')	Protestants ('new religion')	Puritans (strict Protestants)
Beliefs	The pope is the head of the Church helped by cardinals, bishops and priests.	No pope. It may be necessary to have archbishops or bishops.	No popes, cardinals or bishops.
	Church is the intermediary (go-between) between God and people. Can forgive sins.	Personal direct relationship with God via prayer and Bible. Only God can forgive sins.	
	During Mass bread and wine become actual body and blood of Christ (transubstantiation).	The bread and wine simply represent the body and blood of Christ. There is no miracle.	
	7 sacraments (ceremonies).	2 sacraments: Baptism and Holy Communion.	
	Priests are celibate.	Priests can marry.	
Practices	Services in Latin.	Services in English.	
	Priests wear vestments.	Priests wear simple vestments.	
	Churches highly decorated.	Churches plain and simple.	Churches whitewashed with no decorations.
Support	Catholics the majority in north and west England.	Mostly south-east England (London, Kent, East Anglia).	Puritans found in London and East Anglia.

Now try this

Briefly outline **two** ways in which the beliefs of Catholics, Protestants and Puritans differed in 1558.

Elizabeth's religious settlement

Elizabeth's religious settlement (1559) aimed to establish a form of religion that would be acceptable to both Protestants and Catholics.

Key features of Elizabeth's religious settlement of 1559

The Act of Uniformity established the appearance of churches and how religious services were to be held. It required everyone to attend church.

The Act of Supremacy: Elizabeth became Supreme Governor (Head) of the Church of England. All clergy and royal officials had to swear an oath of allegiance to her.

An Ecclesiastical High Commission was established to keep discipline within the Church and enforce Elizabeth's religious settlement. Disloyal clergy could be punished.

Elizabeth's religious settlement

The Royal Injunctions: This was a set of instructions to the clergy that reinforced the Acts of Supremacy and Uniformity. It included instructions on how people should worship God and how religious services were to be conducted.

The Book of Common Prayer (1559) introduced a set church service to be used in all churches. The clergy had to follow the Prayer Book wording during services or be punished.

Ecclesiastical means anything to do with the Church.

The aims of Elizabeth's religious settlement

Elizabeth's religious settlement was inclusive and designed to be accepted by as many of her subjects as possible. Therefore, the wording of the new Prayer Book could be understood to mean different things by Catholics and Protestants.

- The Communion Sacrament referred to in the Book of Common Prayer could be interpreted as the body and blood of Jesus (transubstantiation). This would have appealed to Catholics, while Protestants could view it as an act of remembrance.

- Protestants would have approved of the ban on pilgrimages to 'fake' miracles, while Catholics would have approved of the possibility of 'real miracles.'

- Catholics would also have approved of the use of candles, crosses and vestments in church services.

Impacts of the religious settlement

- 8000 clergy out of about 10 000 accepted the religious settlement.

- Many Marian Bishops (Catholic Bishops appointed by Mary Tudor) opposed the settlement and had to be replaced.

- The majority of ordinary people accepted Elizabeth's religious settlement and attended the church services, even though many of them held on to Catholic beliefs.

The Royal Injunctions

These stated that all clergy were required to:

- teach the Royal Supremacy

- report those refusing to attend church to the Privy Council – absentees were fined a week's wages

- keep a copy of the Bible in English

- have a government licence to preach

- prevent pilgrimages, religious shrines and monuments to 'fake' miracles

- wear special clothes (vestments).

Now try this

1 Describe **two** ways in which the Elizabethan religious settlement affected the Church.

2 Give **two** reasons why a Protestant would have been happy with Elizabeth's religious settlement of 1559.

Church of England: its role in society

The Church of England played an important role in national government, and in town and village life.

Preached the government's message – priests needed a government's licence to preach. This ensured the clergy preached Elizabeth's religious and political message, as those who refused to do so would be denied a licence.

Provided guidance for communities – the parish church helped people in times of hardship and uncertainty.

Enforced Elizabeth's religious settlement of 1559.

Role of the Church of England in society

Responsible for Church Courts – these dealt with marriage, sexual offences, slander (false insults), wills and inheritance.

Find out more about the religious settlement on page 8.

Legitimised Elizabeth's rule – the Church encouraged people to remain loyal to and not rebel against their monarch.

Visitations – bishops carried out inspections of churches and clergy, to ensure they obeyed the religious settlement. These took place every 3–4 years. Visitations also involved checking the licences of physicians, midwives and surgeons.

Role of parish clergy in village life

- In all parishes the clergyman was a major figure in the village community and conducted church services including baptisms, weddings and funerals.

- The clergy offered spiritual and practical advice and guidance to people, especially when times were difficult (such as during a poor harvest).

- The clergy were funded by taxes or **tithes**, or by other sources of income, such as the sale of church pews. The gentry funded some parishes while others remained independent of local landowners.

A tithe was a tax worth 10% of people's income or goods produced.

Role of parish clergy in town life

- Parish churches in towns contained a much wider collection of people, including merchants, craftsmen, labourers and vagrants. There was often a wider range of religious beliefs, too, especially in London, which contained mainstream Protestants, Puritans and Catholics.

- The role of the clergy varied both within towns and between them. In London a wide variety of parishes existed, some of which were very wealthy while others were relatively poor.

- Due to overcrowding, parish clergy in towns had a wider range of issues to deal with than was the case in rural parishes. These included poverty, vagrancy and diseases, such as smallpox and plague.

Now try this

1 In what ways did the Church of England control Elizabethan society?
2 Explain the role played by the clergy in rural parishes between 1558 and 1588.

9

The Puritan challenge

Many radical protestants, or Puritans, challenged Elizabeth's religious settlement of 1559. However, by the late 1560s most Protestant clergy were doing as the queen required.

Who were the Puritans?

Puritans were radical Protestants who wanted to 'purify' the Christian religion by getting rid of anything that wasn't in the Bible.

Vestments were special clothing worn by clergy during worship.

- Puritans wanted to develop their own Church, which would not be controlled by the queen. There would be no bishops, and priests would not wear **vestments**.

- Puritans wanted to make the world a 'more godly' place by banning 'sinful' activities, such as gambling and cock fighting.

- Puritans wanted a simpler style of worship, whitewashed churches and no 'graven images' (worship of religious idols), including crucifixes and statues, which were seen as ungodly and too Catholic.

- A minority of Puritans believed the monarch could be overthrown in certain circumstances. This was especially the case if the monarch was Catholic.

A Puritan family – the father is teaching his wife and children.

- Many Puritans were anti-Catholic and believed the pope was the 'anti-Christ'. Other Puritans – **millenarians** – believed the world was ending and that Christians had to prepare for Jesus' return.

The nature of the Puritan challenge

Crucifixes: Elizabeth, anxious not to upset her Catholic subjects, demanded that a crucifix be placed in each church.

↓

Puritans opposed this, and, when some Puritan bishops threatened to resign, Elizabeth backed down, as she could not replace them with educated Protestant clergy of similar ability.

Vestments: Elizabeth wanted the clergy to wear special vestments, as described in the Royal Injunctions. Puritans resisted this, arguing that clergy should either wear no vestments or simple vestments. In 1566 the Archbishop of Canterbury, Thomas Parker, required priests in his Book of Advertisements to attend an exhibition showing the vestments they must wear.

↓

This resulted in the resignation of 37 Puritan priests, who refused to attend church and to wear the new vestments as required.

The extent of the Puritan challenge

- Puritans were a vocal group within English society. Puritans, such as John Foxe, Thomas Cartwright and John Field, were openly anti-Catholic and opposed to bishops.

- While Puritans were active in London, Cambridge, Oxford and parts of East Anglia, Puritanism had less of an impact on northern England, where people remained mostly Catholic in outlook.

- The government ignored Puritan demands for reform of the Church of England, including the Admonition to Parliament in 1572, suggesting that Puritanism's support was limited.

Now try this

Briefly describe **two** ways in which the Puritans challenged Elizabeth's religious settlement.

The Catholic challenge at home

The Catholic Church became increasingly hostile to Protestantism and Elizabeth's rule.

The Counter Reformation

The Catholic Church's attempt to reverse the Protestant Reformation in Europe and stop its spread was known as the Counter Reformation. Protestants in Europe were charged with **heresy**.

In 1566, the pope issued an instruction to English Catholics to not attend Church of England services.

Heresy involves denying the teachings of the Catholic Church. The Catholic Church dealt with heretics severely, with many being executed for their beliefs.

Timeline

1534 Act of Supremacy: the king and not the pope is head of the Church of England.

1559 Elizabeth's religious settlement.

1517 Start of the Reformation under Martin Luther.

1553–58 Catholicism is restored under Mary Tudor.

1545–63 Council of Trent and Counter Reformation leads to determination to reverse gains made by Protestantism in Europe and England since Reformation.

The nature of the Catholic threat at home

Counter Reformation in Europe attempts to reverse the spread of Protestantism. → Catholic hostility towards Protestants. →

- The pope instructs English Catholics not to attend Church of England services.
- One-third of the English nobility and a large part of the gentry are **recusants**.

→ Revolt of the Northern Earls (1569–70).

Recusants practised the Catholic religion in secret. Elizabeth tolerated them initially, as she did not want to turn them into religious martyrs (people prepared to die for their religion) and to avoid a Catholic rebellion.

The extent of the Catholic threat

- Up to one-third of the nobility (major landowners) and many gentry (smaller landowners) were recusants, especially in the north and northwest England.
- Catholic nobility tended to be from traditional and powerful families that had prospered under Mary Tudor, such as the Nevilles and the Percys. They resented their loss of influence under Elizabeth and disliked the growing influence of her favourites, such as Sir William Cecil and Robert Dudley, Earl of Leicester, who they saw as Protestant upstarts.
- The nobility in the north were very influential and had always enjoyed freedom of action (independence) from the Crown, so they were well placed to incite a rebellion against Elizabeth.
- This threat was increased by the pope's instruction that Catholics were not to attend Church of England services. This gave them a powerful religious reason to rebel.

Burning Protestant books during the Counter Reformation.

Now try this

Remember this is a 'why' question, so you must give reasons.

Explain why many Catholics opposed Elizabeth's religious settlement.

The Catholic challenge abroad

Many of Europe's most powerful rulers tended to be Catholic and, encouraged by the pope, represented a real threat to Queen Elizabeth's monarchy, as they could seek to remove her from the throne and replace her with a Catholic monarch.

Extent of Catholic challenge from abroad in 1570

Key
▨ Territory controlled by Europe's Catholic powers

By 1570, Elizabeth was surrounded by potentially hostile Catholic powers that could seek to overthrow her and replace her with a Catholic monarch.

France

When religious war began in France, in 1562, Elizabeth backed French Protestants, hoping to take back Calais in return. Yet this policy failed, as French Protestants made peace with the Catholics later that year.

> Elizabeth could not afford to upset both France and Spain, as this would increase threats to her throne.

The papacy

The Counter Reformation meant the pope was prepared to end Protestant rule in England. He disapproved of the steps that Elizabeth had taken to suppress Catholicism following the revolt of the Northern Earls.

The pope had already **excommunicated** Elizabeth in 1570. This could only encourage Catholic powers, such as France and Spain, to attack England.

> **Excommunication** means being formally excluded from the Catholic Church and unable to receive its sacraments.

Spain

- In 1566 the Dutch rebelled against Spanish occupation. Elizabeth outwardly condemned the Dutch rebels, known as the Sea Beggars, but many made their way to England. Spanish atrocities against Protestants (hundreds were put to death in the Netherlands) put Elizabeth under pressure to shelter rebels, who attacked Spanish ships in the Channel.
- Spain was further angered by England's seizure of the Genoese loan in 1568. The Italian city of Genoa lent gold to the Spanish government. Ships carrying the loan sheltered in English ports, where Elizabeth seized it, arguing it belonged to Italian bankers not Spain.
- By 1570, Spanish rule in the Netherlands was secure. The Privy Council now feared a Spanish invasion, as Spanish troops were in the Spanish Netherlands close to England (see map).
- The presence of Mary, Queen of Scots, as an alternative Catholic monarch encouraged the Spanish government to plot against Elizabeth.

> For more on the Revolt of the Northern Earls, 1569–70, turn to page 18.

> For more on England's political and religious rivalry with Spain, see page 23.

> For more on the Counter Reformation, turn to page 11.

> For more on plots against Elizabeth involving Mary, Queen of Scots, turn to pages 19–21.

Now try this

Explain how relations between England and Spain declined between 1560 and 1570.

Mary's claim to the throne and arrival in England

Mary, Queen of Scots, had a legitimate claim to the English throne and was at the centre of many plots designed to overthrow Elizabeth.

Mary's claim to the throne

Mary, Queen of Scots, was Henry VII's great-granddaughter and Elizabeth's second cousin. She was descended from Margaret Tudor, Henry VIII's sister, was Catholic and had a legitimate claim to the English throne. Mary was married to the French king, Francis II, and inherited the Scottish crown when she was only six days old. While Mary was in France, her mother, Mary of Guise, ruled Scotland.

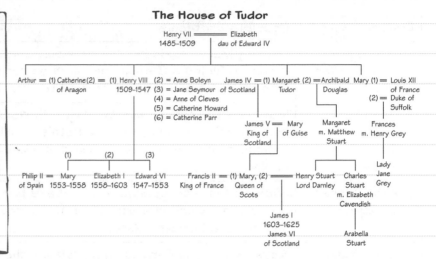

The House of Tudor

Why was Mary important?

* Mary was Catholic, which meant that many Catholics, including members of the nobility, would be prepared to support her claim to the throne.

* Mary's claim was strengthened by the fact there were no concerns about her legitimacy. Elizabeth's legitimacy was questioned by Catholics, however, as her mother Anne Boleyn's marriage to Henry VIII was seen by many Catholics as illegitimate. This undermined Elizabeth's claim to the throne.

* Mary, therefore, would always be at the centre of Catholic plots and conspiracies against Elizabeth. These involved both English plotters and foreign powers.

For more information, see pages 15–17.

Mary leaves Scotland

On the death of Francis II in 1560, Mary returned to Scotland and married Henry Stuart (Lord Darnley), producing an heir, James. Darnley was subsequently murdered (possibly with Mary's involvement) and this time Mary married the Earl of Bothwell.

Many Scots assumed that Mary had murdered Darnley and, in 1568, they rebelled against her, imprisoned her and forced her to abdicate (give up her throne) in favour of her son, James. Mary escaped and raised an army, but this was defeated at Langside near Glasgow. Mary subsequently fled to England, seeking her cousin Elizabeth's help against the Scottish rebels.

Mary's imprisonment in England, 1568

Mary was held in England in comfort but under guard while Elizabeth decided what to do with her. The Scottish rebels demanded that Mary be handed over and tried for the murder of Darnley.

Mary's arrival in England created a problem for Elizabeth. By remaining in England she could encourage rebellion, as many members of the Catholic nobility believed they could overthrow Elizabeth and place Mary on the throne. However, to take action against Mary, as an anointed monarch, would also reduce Elizabeth's own status, power and authority.

Turn to pages 16–17 for more on plots against Elizabeth involving Mary, Queen of Scots.

Now try this

Briefly explain why Mary, Queen of Scots, was imprisoned in England in 1568.

Mary vs Elizabeth

Relations between the two monarchs remained tense, as Elizabeth became increasingly concerned about the presence of Mary, Queen of Scots, in England between 1568 and 1569, and the threat she posed to her throne.

Elizabeth's options with Mary, Queen of Scots, in 1568–69

Option	Possible problems
1 Help Mary to regain her throne	Helping Mary regain her throne would anger the Scottish nobility and leave Elizabeth facing a Catholic monarch on her northern border. The Auld Alliance with France could then be revived to threaten her.
2 Hand Mary over to the Scottish lords	Mary was the former wife of Francis II. Her trial, imprisonment and execution by Scottish noblemen with Elizabeth's permission could provoke France, driving them into alliance with Spain, which could lead both countries into war with England.
3 Allow Mary to go abroad	Allowing Mary to go abroad could see her return to France. This could provoke a French plot that aimed to remove Elizabeth from the English throne and replace her with Mary.
4 Keep Mary in England	Keeping Mary in England was probably the best option for Elizabeth. However, it carried the risk that Catholic plotters might try to overthrow Elizabeth and replace her with Mary.

The Casket Letters Affair

- A meeting was set up at York to hear the case against Mary between October 1568 and January 1569.
- The Scottish lords brought love letters with them, apparently demonstrating that Mary was guilty of murdering Lord Darnley.
- Mary said that she could not be tried because she was an anointed monarch, and would not offer a plea unless Elizabeth guaranteed a verdict of innocence.
- Elizabeth refused, but she did not hand over Mary for trial.

By not handing over Mary, Elizabeth ensured:

- 👍 the Scottish nobility would not imprison or execute Mary
- 👍 the French would be satisfied
- 👍 her subjects did not punish an anointed monarch.

The conference did not reach any conclusions. Mary, therefore, stayed in England, in captivity. But she remained a threat to Elizabeth, because any plots against her, especially those involving Catholics, would seek to replace Elizabeth with Mary.

Why did Elizabeth not make Mary her heir?

One further possibility was that Elizabeth would acknowledge Mary as her heir. However, to do so would upset English Protestants, including those on her Privy Council. Without the support of these Privy Councillors, Elizabeth – already distrusted by many Catholics – would have few supporters left. Moreover, the prospect of a Catholic heir would, in the event of Elizabeth's death, result in civil war.

Now try this

Explain why Mary, Queen of Scots, posed a threat to Elizabeth's position as queen.

The Revolt of the Northern Earls

The Revolt of the Northern Earls (1569–70) was a key turning point in Elizabeth's reign.

Why did the Northern Earls rebel?

- The earls and their followers wanted to make England Catholic again. They especially resented the appointment of James Pilkington, a Protestant, as Bishop of Durham in 1561.
- The earls had lost much of their influence at court under Elizabeth. They resented the 'new men', such as William Cecil, John Forster and Robert Dudley.
- Elizabeth's refusal to name an heir, or to marry and have a child, created uncertainty. The earls feared civil war and loss of power and wealth under a future Protestant monarch.

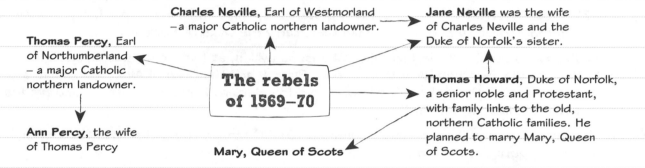

Charles Neville, Earl of Westmorland –a major Catholic northern landowner.

Jane Neville was the wife of Charles Neville and the Duke of Norfolk's sister.

Thomas Percy, Earl of Northumberland – a major Catholic northern landowner.

The rebels of 1569–70

Thomas Howard, Duke of Norfolk, a senior noble and Protestant, with family links to the old, northern Catholic families. He planned to marry Mary, Queen of Scots.

Ann Percy, the wife of Thomas Percy

Mary, Queen of Scots

The marriage plan

- Mary would marry the Duke of Norfolk, depose (remove) Elizabeth and become queen herself. She told the Spanish Ambassador in 1569 that she "shall be Queen of England in three months" and that "mass shall be said all over the country".
- Robert Dudley told Elizabeth of the plot, leading to Norfolk's arrest and imprisonment in the Tower.

Progress of the revolt

- Northumberland and Westmorland, with their wives' support, continued with the revolt. They took control of Durham Cathedral, celebrating mass there, as well as in other northern churches, and began to move south.
- Elizabeth moved Mary to Coventry, to stop her escaping to join the rebels.
- Though the rebels captured Hartlepool, support from Spain never arrived.

Why did the revolt fail?

- Support from Spain never arrived.
- Many northern landowners, especially those in Lancashire and Cheshire, remained loyal to Elizabeth.
- Many landowners did not want to risk losing wealth gained from the dissolution of the monasteries under Henry VIII by backing a failed revolt.

The revolt's significance

- It showed Mary, Queen of Scots, could not be trusted – and she remained in prison.
- The pope excommunicated Elizabeth and called on loyal Catholics to depose her. This encouraged further Catholic plots against her.
- The loyalty of England's Catholics was now in doubt, forcing the government to take harsh steps against them.
- Elizabeth's control over the north of England was strengthened.

Now try this

Think about Catholics and Spain.

1 Why did the Northern Revolt threaten Elizabeth's position as monarch in 1569–70?
2 Did the defeat of the revolt in 1570 strengthen or weaken Elizabeth's grip on power?

The Ridolfi plot

The Ridolfi plot was one of a number of Catholic plots against Elizabeth after 1570.

Background to the plot

The failure of the revolt of the Northern Earls and the Papal Bull of 1570 meant that Elizabeth and her Privy Council treated Catholics with suspicion.	The Earl of Huntingdon, a committed Protestant, led the Council of the North. He implemented laws against Catholics in the north of England. This angered many Catholics, who were now prepared, with the pope's backing, to plot against Elizabeth.	The Ridolfi plot (1571)

The progress of the Ridolfi plot

1. Roberto Ridolfi was an Italian banker who lived in England and worked as a spy for the pope.

2. In 1571, Ridolfi plotted to murder Elizabeth, start a Spanish invasion and put Mary, Queen of Scots, on the English throne. Mary would then marry the Duke of Norfolk.

3. In March 1571, Ridolfi travelled to the Netherlands (which, at that point, was Spanish controlled) to discuss the plot with the pope, Philip II and the Duke of Alba. Ridolfi had a letter signed by the Duke of Norfolk in which Norfolk declared himself a Catholic and pledged to lead the rebellion with Philip II's support.

4. Philip II instructed the Duke of Alba to prepare 10 000 troops to send across the English Channel in support of the revolt.

5. Sir William Cecil discovered the plot and, by autumn 1571, was able to prove that Norfolk was guilty of high treason (plotting against Elizabeth). Ridolfi remained abroad and never returned to England.

6. When parliament reconvened in May 1572, it demanded the execution of both Norfolk and Mary, Queen of Scots. Elizabeth signed Norfolk's death warrant leading to his execution in June 1572. Yet Elizabeth was reluctant to punish Mary, and even refused to remove her from the succession.

Elizabeth had to proceed cautiously. Executing Mary would further anger English Catholics and possibly unite France and Spain (Europe's two big Catholic monarchies) against her.

It reinforced the threat from Spain, as Philip II would support any plots against Elizabeth.

It confirmed that English Catholics and Mary, Queen of Scots, remained a threat to Elizabeth.

The significance of the Ridolfi plot

The threat from Spain meant that England needed to improve relations with France, as England could not fight both countries at once.

The government now began to monitor Catholics more closely and treat them more severely. Two laws passed in 1581 meant that families could be fined for sheltering priests and charged with treason if they converted people to Catholicism.

Now try this

Briefly explain why the Ridolfi plot was a threat to Elizabeth I.

The Throckmorton and Babington plots

The Throckmorton and Babington plots were organised by Catholics against Elizabeth.

The Throckmorton plot, 1583

The French Duke of Guise, a cousin of Mary, Queen of Scots, plotted to invade England and overthrow Elizabeth, free Mary and make England Catholic again.

- Philip II offered to help pay for the revolt and the pope approved of the conspiracy.
- Francis Throckmorton, a young Englishman, would pass letters between the plotters and Mary, Queen of Scots.

The failure of the Throckmorton plot

- Sir Francis Walsingham, Elizabeth's Secretary of State, discovered the plot in May 1583.
- In November 1583, Walsingham's spies found papers at Throckmorton's house that revealed his part in the conspiracy.
- Throckmorton was arrested and tortured. He confessed to his involvement and was executed in May 1584.

Why was the Throckmorton plot significant?

Significance of Throckmorton plot	→	Revealed extent of threat posed by foreign Catholic powers, English Catholics and Mary, Queen of Scots.	→	Showed potential threat from France and Spain. Elizabeth had to take care these Catholic powers did not unite against her.
		Throckmorton's papers included a list of Catholic sympathisers in England, confirming government's fears of 'enemy within'.	→	Government treated English Catholics with greater suspicion. Many fled England after the plot. Up to 11 000 were imprisoned, or kept under surveillance or house arrest. An Act of Parliament of 1585 made helping or sheltering Catholic priests punishable with death.

The Babington plot (1586) and the execution of Mary, Queen of Scots

1. The Duke of Guise would invade England, murder Elizabeth and put Mary, Queen of Scots, on the throne. Philip II and the pope supported the plot.
2. Anthony Babington, a Catholic, wrote to Mary in July 1586 about the conspiracy.
3. Sir Francis Walsingham intercepted and read Babington's letters to Mary, which clearly demonstrated her awareness of, support for and involvement in the conspiracy.
4. Babington and the plotters were sentenced to death and hanged, drawn and quartered.
5. In October 1586, Mary was sentenced to death for her part in the plot. Elizabeth delayed, but signed Mary's death warrant in February 1587. Mary was beheaded shortly afterwards.

In quo quis peccat In eo punitur.

Why was the Babington plot significant?

- Elizabeth's situation was more precarious than with previous plots.
- By 1585, England and Spain were virtually at war.
- Elizabeth's government became determined to crush the Catholic threat.
- The persecution of Catholics intensified. In 1585, 11 000 Catholics were imprisoned or placed under house arrest. Thirty-one priests were executed across the country in 1586.
- The plot led to the execution of Mary, Queen of Scots, ending any hope of replacing Elizabeth with a Catholic heir.

The execution of the Babington plotters. The gallows were erected 'mighty high', to be visible to all to deter further plots.

Now try this

Briefly explain why the Babington and Throckmorton plots threatened Elizabeth I.

Walsingham's spies

Sir Francis Walsingham, Elizabeth's Secretary of State, developed a network of spies and informers to uncover plots against Elizabeth.

Why was Sir Francis Walsingham important?

Walsingham, Elizabeth's spymaster

Walsingham's actions provided intelligence that defeated plots, such as the Throckmorton plot and Babington plot.

His intelligence unmasked the activities of Mary, Queen of Scots. This put pressure on Elizabeth to execute her and led to Mary's execution in early 1587.

His actions also deterred further plots against Elizabeth.

Walsingham's spy network

✓ Walsingham had a network of spies and informants in every town.

✓ Some of Walsingham's agents were paid and trained by the government.

✓ Others were paid informants. These were often people who knew or were likely to know potential plotters against the queen. They were sometimes Catholic priests, such as John Hart, who turned informant in return for a Royal Pardon.

✓ Walsingham also used spies abroad. He had agents in France, Germany, Spain, Italy and North Africa.

Walsingham's use of ciphers

Walsingham used ciphers (codes) for all correspondences. This meant that letters would be written in code and translated out of code once received.

Walsingham also had the means of decoding (deciphering) the codes of those who plotted against Elizabeth. He hired specialists, such as Thomas Phelippes, to help him do this.

For more on Walsingham's role in uncovering the Throckmorton and Babington plots against Elizabeth I, turn to page 17.

Walsingham's use of torture and execution

✓ Some priests were tortured, to deter others and force them to give up information. Under Walsingham, 130 priests and 60 of their supporters were put to death.

✓ The threat of execution and torture was often more effective, as it would provide Walsingham with informants he could use against any plotters.

✓ Walsingham only used torture and execution in the most serious cases, as he did not want ordinary people to sympathise with plotters.

Agents provocateurs

Walsingham employed 'agents provocateurs' to encourage those who were seen as a threat to Elizabeth to plot against her. This justified their arrest and execution.
For example, Walsingham used Gilbert Gifford to open communications between Mary and the Babington plotters. This encouraged Mary to involve herself in the plot, so leading to her execution.

For more on the reasons for the execution of Mary, Queen of Scots, turn to page 19.

Now try this

Why was the government able to defeat Catholic plots between 1570 and 1586?

The execution of Mary, Queen of Scots

Elizabeth I eventually signed Mary's death warrant in February 1587. Mary, Queen of Scots, was executed for a number of different reasons.

Why was Mary, Queen of Scots, executed?

- Mary had been involved in a series of plots against Elizabeth, such as the revolt of the Northern Earls, the Ridolfi plot, the Throckmorton plot and the Babington plot.
- Walsingham's spies had unearthed evidence that Mary was involved with the plotters. This led to her trial and conviction under the Act for Preservation of the Queen's Safety.
- The Spanish threat was very real by 1587, with rumours of invasion. The fact that Philip II had been involved in previous plots involving Mary, such as the Ridolfi plot, heightened the threat that Mary posed and the reasons for getting rid of her.
- Mary remained a rallying point for disgruntled Catholics who saw her as a legitimate queen.
- The pope excommunicated Elizabeth in 1570, making Mary an alternative Catholic monarch who could take the throne by foreign invasion.
- Mary had a (Catholic) son who would be heir to the English throne. This threatened the Protestant succession while creating the possibility of civil war.

Mary was an anointed monarch, so executing her set a dangerous precedent. Elizabeth, in the wrong circumstances, could meet a similar fate. So the execution made Elizabeth and her heirs more vulnerable in the future.

The execution further angered Spain and gave Philip II further reason to attack England, as Mary left her claim to the throne to Philip on her death.

Why was the execution of Mary, Queen of Scots, significant?

The execution left Elizabeth without an heir, increasing the chances of a civil war on her death.

The execution removed an important threat to Elizabeth, as there was now no alternative monarch to replace her.

The execution of Mary, Queen of Scots, on 8 February 1587 at Fotheringhay Castle.

Now try this

Explain **two** reasons why Mary, Queen of Scots, was executed in 1587.

Spain: political and religious rivalry

By the 1580s, relations between England and Spain had reached the point of war.

Religious rivalry

Under Mary Tudor, Spain and England were allies. As a Protestant country under Elizabeth I, England's relationship with Spain soured:

- Philip II, backed by the pope, saw Protestantism as a threat to the authority of the Catholic Church.
- Many English Protestants saw Spain and Catholicism as a threat.
- Philip II of Spain became involved in Catholic plots against Elizabeth.

Spanish policy in the Netherlands

- The Netherlands had been Spanish since the 1400s, but many Dutch became Protestant.
- A brutal Spanish campaign under the Duke of Alba aimed to restore Catholicism there.
- Spanish Catholics executed many Dutch Protestants following the Council of Troubles (the 'Council of Blood') in 1568.
- Spain's campaign in the Netherlands angered many in Elizabeth's government, who now saw Spain as hostile – a direct threat to English Protestantism and to England itself.

The Spanish Fury and the Pacification of Ghent

By 1576, the Spanish government in the Netherlands found the war there unaffordable. A lack of funds meant Spanish troops went unpaid. This resulted in the **Spanish Fury**, when Spanish troops looted Antwerp.

After the looting, all 17 Dutch provinces (Catholic and Protestant) joined an alliance against the Spanish, drawn up in a document called the **Pacification of Ghent**. It called for all Spanish troops to be expelled from the Netherlands.

The English response to the Spanish

Elizabeth's government decided to secretly help Dutch Protestants resist the Spanish.

- It allowed Dutch rebel ships (the Sea Beggars) safe passage in English ports.
- It provided financial support to others fighting the Spanish, including volunteers led by John Casimir, a foreign mercenary.
- English privateers, such as Sir Francis Drake, were encouraged to attack Spanish shipping and colonies in Latin America.

Elizabeth even proposed marriage to the French heir, the Duke of Alençon, so he might be persuaded to fight Spain in the Netherlands.

Restoring Spanish influence

By late 1584:

- Spanish control of the Netherlands had been restored under the Duke of Parma
- England's allies, the Duke of Alençon and William of Orange, were dead
- The Treaty of Joinville (1584) united Catholic France and Spain against the Netherlands and England
- Dutch Catholics were ready to make peace with Spain, strengthening Philip II's position there.

England and Spain close to war

By 1587, England and Spain were close to war.

- Philip II blamed English support of the Dutch rebels for making the situation worse.
- Philip II blamed English **privateers** for attacks on Spanish shipping.
- Elizabeth's government blamed Spain for a series of plots against Elizabeth.

Privateers were sailors on privately owned warships who attacked Spanish shipping. Because the ships were privately owned, Elizabeth could deny responsibility for their actions.

Now try this

1 Explain **two** reasons why relations between England and Spain deteriorated between 1566 and 1587.

2 How far was Elizabeth's government to blame for the declining relations between England and Spain?

Focus on religious and other reasons, such as the war in the Netherlands and English privateers.

Consider what Elizabeth's government did to make relations worse, for example.

Spain: commercial rivalry

England and Spain had a growing commercial rivalry by the 1570s. It involved trade and the New World, which was affected by English privateering.

Commercial rivalry

By the 1570s, England and Spain had emerged as commercial (trade) rivals. Both competed against each other for access to the markets and resources of the New World, as well as to markets in Turkey, Europe, Russia, China and North Africa.
Spain had conquered Mexico and Peru in the early 1500s. This provided the Spanish government with vast amounts of gold and silver, which were regularly shipped back to Spain. It also gave Spain control over the trade in sugar cane and tobacco.
By Elizabeth's reign, Britain had emerged as a trade rival. Sailors, including Sir Francis Drake, were journeying great distances on trading voyages to different parts of the world.

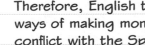

English hostility towards Spain.

Spain represented a major barrier to English trade because:

- Spanish control of the Netherlands and the Scheldt and Rhine estuaries closed off one of the principal trade routes used by English traders in Europe – this reduced the incomes and profits of English merchants

- Spain's control of the New World also denied English traders profit-making opportunities, because all trade there had to be licensed by the Spanish government.

Therefore, English traders' efforts to find ways of making money brought them into conflict with the Spanish government.

Deteriorating relations

By the early 1580s, the actions of Drake and other privateers had brought England and Spain to the brink of war.

- Elizabeth, by knighting Drake, demonstrated her defiance of and hostility towards Spain's commercial interests in Europe and the New World. Her actions showed her support of the financial losses suffered by the Spanish government as a result of English privateering.

- For Philip II, Drake and other privateers were little more than pirates who needed to be removed by war if necessary. So, getting rid of Elizabeth and Drake by war was the only remaining means of protecting Spain's commercial interests.

For more on the Spanish Fury in the Netherlands, which resulted from Spanish soldiers going unpaid, turn to page 20.

Privateering

- English merchants, financed by private investors, including Elizabeth herself, raided Spanish colonies as well as ships voyaging to and from the New World.

- In one raid alone, in 1572, Sir Francis Drake captured £40000 in Spanish silver.

- A second expedition between 1577 and 1580, involving Drake's circumnavigation of the globe, resulted in the capture of a further £400000 of silver and gold.

- Elizabeth also encouraged Dutch rebels, known as the Sea Beggars, to attack Spanish ships sailing between Spain and the Netherlands.

- By 1580, loss of silver meant that the Spanish government in the Netherlands was bankrupt and could not afford to pay its soldiers.

Now try this

Briefly explain **two** ways in which commercial rivalry led England and Spain to the brink of war by 1585.

The Netherlands and Cadiz

By 1585, Elizabeth began to support the Dutch rebels directly by sending troops to the Netherlands under Robert Dudley, Earl of Leicester. Francis Drake continued to attack Spanish shipping and raided the Spanish fleet at Cadiz.

Background to the war with Spain

England signed the Treaty of Nonsuch in August 1585 with the Dutch Protestant rebels. This made war with Spain more likely. By the terms of the treaty, England would pay for an army of 7,400 English soldiers, led by an English commander – Robert Dudley, Earl of Leicester – who would work with the rebels' government, the Council of State. It was likely that this group would fight the Spanish, although war had not been formally declared.

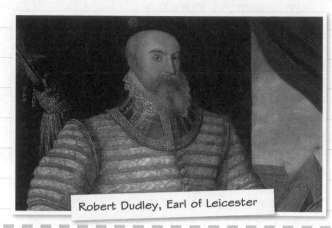

Robert Dudley, Earl of Leicester

The campaign in the Netherlands (1585–88)

The campaign was not a great success:

- **Elizabeth still hoped to negotiate with Philip II.** England was not formally at war with Spain and so Leicester was not given enough resources to defeat the Spanish.
- **Some of Dudley's officers,** William Stanley and Robert York, **defected to the Spanish side.** This damaged relations with the Dutch rebels.
- **Dudley and Elizabeth had different aims in the Netherlands.** Dudley wanted to end Spanish rule, making the Netherlands an independent country. Elizabeth wanted to go back to how the Netherlands had been governed in 1548 when it remained under Spanish control but with certain freedoms given to it.

The results of the campaign

The campaign achieved very little:

- Dudley could only disrupt Spanish forces in the Netherlands under the Duke of Parma. He could not defeat them.
- Dudley did manage to stop the Spanish from capturing a deep-water port, Ostend, on the English Channel. This was important because it denied the Spanish Armada the chance to link up with the Duke of Parma's troops in 1588.

To read more about the Spanish Armada of 1588, turn to pages 23–25.

Drake's attack on Cadiz: 'Singeing the King of Spain's beard'

- Since January 1586, Spain had been gradually building up its Armada, Philip II's enormous invasion fleet that was due to help the Spanish army invade England.
- In March 1587, Elizabeth ordered Francis Drake to attack the Spanish navy. Between 19 and 22 April, he attacked Cadiz, a major Spanish naval port, destroying 30 ships and much of the fleet's supplies. This attack was called the 'singeing of the King of Spain's beard'.
- Drake then continued to attack Spanish coastal ports and treasure ships.

The importance of Drake's attacks on Cadiz and Spain

- Spain had to take a break from building the Armada in order to defend itself against Drake.
- The disruption Drake caused did not stop the Armada, but it delayed it by a year.
- This bought England more time to prepare for the eventual Spanish attack and invasion in 1588.

Now try this

Why was Drake's attack on Cadiz important?

Spanish invasion plans

Philip II had a range of different reasons for launching the Spanish Armada.

Why did Philip launch the Spanish Armada?

Religious conflict

- Philip II, a devout Catholic, had already failed in plots to get rid of Elizabeth. The Armada and invasion gave him another opportunity to remove her and place a Catholic on the English throne.
- The papacy had wanted to overthrow Elizabeth since excommunicating her in 1570.
- The pope promised absolution (forgiveness of sins) to those taking part in the Armada.

Politics and diplomacy

- The Treaty of Joinville (1584) meant Spain could attack England without risking war with France.
- The Treaty of Nonsuch (1585) meant English soldiers were at war with Spain, so Philip could justify attacking England.
- England would be a useful addition to Philip's empire, as it would give Spain complete control of the Atlantic.

Philip II launched the Spanish Armada in 1588.

Acts of provocation

- Drake's actions in the New World threatened Spanish commercial interests.
- Elizabeth's support for Dutch rebels challenged Spanish interests there.

Changing circumstances

- Spain acquired Portugal in 1580, giving Philip II access to Portuguese ports and ships.
- The Duke of Parma's success in the Netherlands since 1579 meant Spain's position there was secure.
- Elizabeth's hesitation to fully back Dutch rebels was a sign of weakness and encouraged Philip II to attack.

Philip II's strategy

- Philip ordered the Armada (130 ships and 2431 guns) to sail along the English Channel to the Netherlands.
- From there, the ships would join forces with Spanish troops under the Duke of Parma and transport 27 000 troops to Kent.
- The Spanish army would then attack London, end Elizabeth's reign and establish a new Catholic government.

Tactics

- For the invasion to succeed, the Spanish needed control of the English Channel to transport Parma's troops to England.
- It was vital that the English Navy disrupt Spanish shipping, as the Spanish had a bigger and better army than the English and were likely to defeat them if they landed successfully in Kent.

Why was the Armada such a threat?

If the Armada succeeded, Elizabeth could lose her throne and possibly her life.

For English Protestants, including her privy councillors, a successful invasion meant the restoration of Catholicism in England and the persecution of Protestants. For many, the war with Spain was a life and death struggle to preserve their religion and their lives.

Now try this

Explain **two** reasons why Philip II launched the Spanish Armada in 1588.

Choose two of the four headings in the diagram at the top of this page. Try to explain how they encouraged Philip II to launch his Armada.

Reasons for the English victory

The Spanish Armada was defeated for a number of reasons.

What happened to the Armada of 1588?

29 July – the Armada is spotted in the English Channel.

31 July – Battle of Plymouth. Two Spanish ships are captured.

3–4 August – Battle of the Isle of Wight. Spanish ships are outgunned by the English and forced to move further up the channel towards Calais.

8 August – Battle of Gravelines. Fireships cause the Spanish to panic. The Spanish fleet never links up with the Duke of Parma and is scattered.

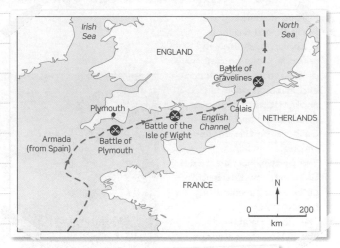

The course of the Spanish Armada, 1588.

Communication problems:
- There was no communication between the Duke of Parma and the Duke of Medina-Sidonia.
- No deep-water ports. The Dutch rebels still possessed Ostend. This meant the Spanish Armada could not stop at any ports in the Spanish Netherlands, but had to meet up with the Duke of Parma's army at sea after it had embarked on a series of smaller ships. This made communications very difficult.

Spanish ships lacked supplies and provisions, including food, for a long voyage.
The Spanish fleet was at sea for 10 weeks and by early August the food had rotted. This damaged Spanish morale and their ability to fight the English.

Reasons for the English victory

English ships were better armed and equipped.
In English ships, cannons were mounted on smaller gun carriages than on Spanish ships. This meant they could be reloaded and fired more quickly than the Spanish cannons. This damaged many Spanish ships and undermined their chances of linking up with the Duke of Parma and invading England.

The Spanish panicked.
The key turning point seems to have been the Battle of Gravelines, where the English used fireships. Many Spanish captains panicked, cut their anchors and allowed their ships to drift into the North Sea.

English tactics were superior:
- The English got close enough to the Spanish ships to fire on them, but stayed far away enough to prevent Spanish sailors and soldiers from boarding. This destroyed and damaged a number of Spanish ships while ensuring that English losses were minimal.
- Drake's use of fireships at the Battle of Gravelines was also important as it caused the Spanish to panic.

The weather.
Gale force winds caused most of the destruction to the Spanish ships as they retreated home. Many Spanish ships were destroyed off the west of Ireland.

Now try this

Explain **two** reasons why the Spanish Armada was defeated in 1588.

 Use the information in the diagram above to help you answer this question.

Consequences of the English victory

The English victory over Spain had a number of consequences – for England and for Spain.

English navy strengthened.
The defeat of the Armada showed the strength of the English Navy. This boosted English confidence to explore. It also encouraged English merchants to trade with Europe.

Protestant cause stronger in England.
Victory of the English 'underdog' suggested that God was on the Protestant side. A commemorative medal was struck that said "God blew and they were scattered". This may have persuaded some Englishmen, who might have wavered between Protestantism and Catholicism, to accept Protestant rule.

Consequences of the English victory for England

Elizabeth's authority enhanced.
The queen took centre stage at a victory parade in London. Elizabeth was able to portray herself as a military victor. This is reflected in portraits during the later parts of her reign.

Foreign policy: stronger alliances in Europe.
The Anglo Dutch alliance was strengthened. Protestantism in the Netherlands survived, strengthening the Protestant cause in Europe. This meant England had Protestant allies in Europe and was no longer isolated.

Consequences of the English victory for Spain

- The defeat of the Armada was a major military and financial setback for King Philip II of Spain.

- However, Spain's war with England continued for the rest of Elizabeth's reign.

- Spanish prestige was broken. Other countries became more willing to challenge Spain's power. This led to the gradual decline of the Spanish Empire.

The 'Armada portrait' shows Elizabeth I surrounded by symbols of power with the defeated Armada in the background.

Now try this

How far do you agree that it was the defeat of the Armada that finally secured Elizabeth's position as queen?

Think about the information above, but also consider other events, such as the execution of Mary, Queen of Scots.

Elizabethan education

During Elizabeth's reign, education slowly became more important.

Attitudes towards education

Elizabethan England had no national system of education. The purpose of education was to help people prepare for their expected roles in life, so it was focused on practical skills and possibly basic literacy – only an estimated 15–20% of the population could read and write.

Very few children actually went to school and all schools had fees. The view was that only the rich needed to attend. People saw no need to provide a formal education for the vast majority of the population, especially the labouring classes.

Changing influences on education

- By the early 1500s, philosophers called Humanists were arguing that education was valuable and not merely a way of preparing people for a role in life. This meant educational opportunities gradually improved during Elizabeth's reign.

- Protestants argued that people ought to be able to study the scriptures. This required people to be able to read, boosting literacy.

- The growth of the printing press meant books became less expensive, giving people more opportunities to read.

- The growth of trade in the Elizabethan era required ordinary people to be able to read, write and understand mathematics so they could record transactions properly. This encouraged more people to become literate.

Parish schools (up to age 10): Set up locally by the Church and run by the clergy. Taught basic literacy to the children of yeoman farmers and craftsmen.

Private tutors: Delivered education privately to members of the nobility, who often finished their education in the household of another noble family.

Grammar schools (for boys aged 10 to 14): Provided an education independently of the Church and charged fees, although scholarships were available for poorer families. Attended by the children of the gentry, merchants, yeoman farmers and craftsmen. Boys were taught the Bible, debating, Latin, French, Greek and philosophy. The sons of yeomen farmers and craftsmen were taught reading, writing and mathematics.

Elizabethan education

Petty schools (up to age 10): Run privately from people's homes. Attended by children of the gentry, merchants, yeoman farmers and craftsmen.

Universities (ages 14 to 15 onwards): In Elizabethan England there were two universities: Oxford and Cambridge. There you studied geometry, music, astronomy, philosophy, logic and rhetoric (persuasive speaking used in law), medicine, law and divinity. The highest possible university qualification was the doctorate.

Educating girls

Many girls received no formal education at all as it was felt that they would not need it. Girls from better off families attended Dame Schools run by wealthy women in their homes. Wealthy girls had private tutors.

Changes in education, 1558–88

- New grammar schools meant children were now educated independently of the Church. Scholarships allowed people from poorer backgrounds to receive an education.

- Literacy improved, especially in the towns. This was the combined result of the printing press, parish schools and the need to read the scriptures.

Now try this

1 Explain **two** reasons why education changed during Elizabeth I's reign.
2 Briefly explain **two** key features of grammar schools.

Sport, pastimes and the theatre

There were a number of leisure pursuits in Elizabethan England that were based on social class.

Leisure in Elizabethan England

Social class	Leisure/Pastime	Description
Nobility	Hunting	Took place on horseback with hounds or with birds (hawking). Involved men and women.
	Fishing	Done by men and women.
	Real Tennis	Played indoors (men only). A cross between modern tennis and squash that was increasingly popular.
	Bowls	Similar to the modern game (men only).
	Fencing	Undertaken with blunted swords (men only).
Farmers, craftsmen and the lower classes	Football	Men only. The aim was to get the ball into the other side's goal, although the rules varied. No limit on the numbers involved or the size of the pitch. Could be very violent – men were often killed during matches.
	Wrestling	Men of all classes took part in public wrestling matches with people gambling on the outcome.

Spectator sports in Elizabethan England

Sport	Description
Baiting	Involved watching animals fight to the death. Typically, dogs were encouraged to attack chained bears and bulls, and bets were made on the outcomes of fights.
Cock-fighting	Cockerels attacked each other using metal spurs and their beaks. In many small towns, special arenas were built for cock-fighting. Money was bet on the outcomes of these fights.

Literature and the theatre

- A lot of new literature was written during Elizabeth's reign, although medieval literature, such as Chaucer's *Canterbury Tales*, remained popular.
- Mystery Plays, popular with many Catholics, were replaced with new non-religious (secular) plays. These were shown in purpose-built theatres, such as the Red Lion, the Globe and the Rose.
- Comedies, performed by teams of professional players funded by wealthy noblemen, were very popular. Sponsors included the queen and the Earl of Leicester, and their performers were known as Queen's Men and Leicester's Men.
- All social classes attended the theatre, so purpose-built theatres had to be built to accommodate growing audiences.

Music and dancing

- Many Elizabethans played instruments, including lutes (similar to guitars), spinets and harpsichords (similar to pianos).
- Musical performances were popular. Musicians were paid to play at official functions or public events. Music was also played at fairs and markets, or on public occasions, in churches, taverns, barbers' shops and on the streets. Wealthy families employed their own musicians (always men) to play during meals and feasts. Books of songs were also popular.
- Music was also written to accompany plays performed in public theatres.
- Dancing remained a popular pastime, as it brought together men and women, although the upper and lower classes did not dance together.

Now try this

1 Describe **two** ways in which the lower classes entertained themselves in Elizabethan England.

2 Briefly explain the ways in which the theatre changed during Elizabeth's reign.

The problem of the poor

There were many reasons why poverty and vagabondage increased in Elizabethan England, including population growth, bad harvests, sheep farming and enclosure.

What was poverty during Elizabeth's reign?

- ✓ Spending more than 80% of your income on bread.
- ✓ Being unemployed or ill, so you could no longer provide for yourself or your family.
- ✓ Being unable to afford the rising cost of food.
- ✓ Needing financial help (poor relief) or charity (alms).

Vagrants were people without a settled home or regular work. Many vagrants were also seen as vagabonds – idle and dishonest people who wandered from place to place, committing crimes.

What types of people were poor?

Studies of parish records suggest that the poor fell into the following groupings.

- **Widows or women abandoned by their husbands and their families,** as women were paid very little.
- **The sick and the elderly** who were incapable of work.
- **Orphaned children** – 40% of the poor were under 16 years old.
- **People on low wages.**
- **Itinerants, vagrants and vagabonds** – homeless people who moved from their parishes looking for work. They were often involved in crimes and worried those in authority in Elizabethan England.

Population growth. The population of England grew from 3 million, in 1551, to 4.2 million, by 1601. This increased demand for food (driving up prices) while increasing the labour supply (driving down wages). This meant many ordinary people could no longer provide for themselves or their families.

Growth of towns, such as London and Norwich, drove up the cost of rents, while food prices rose as food had to be brought in from rural areas to be sold.

Bad harvests (in 1562, 1565, 1573 and 1586) hit subsistence farmers (those who ate what they grew), reduced the food supply and drove up prices.

Reasons for poverty in Elizabethan England

Economic recessions caused by trade embargos, such as those involving Spain over the Netherlands, created unemployment and poverty.

Increasing demand for land. As the population increased more people needed land. This drove up rents and resulted in entry fees (up-front sums paid at the start of land rental). Many people could not afford to pay these.

Sheep farming. The growth of the wool trade meant that many farmers preferred to rear sheep, rather than grow food.

Enclosure. Land was divided into fields for animal husbandry, arable farming or both ('up and down farming') and given to farmers who farmed for profit. This denied people use of common land (land that could be used by everyone), which meant they were unable to provide for their families.

Monasteries had provided help for the poor until their dissolution under Henry VIII in the 1530s. Now those struggling had no support.

Enclosure drove many people off the land altogether, leaving them with nowhere to live or farm. They became itinerants and vagrants.

Now try this

How important was population growth in causing poverty in Elizabethan England?

You need to consider other causes of poverty as well as population growth to answer this question.

Changing attitudes

The Elizabethan government responded to the problem of poverty in different ways and, over time, attitudes towards the poor changed.

Changing attitudes towards the poor

Attitudes towards the poor changed during Elizabethan times. There were various reasons for this:

- the fear that poverty led to disorder and was a potential cause of rebellion
- the cost of dealing with the poor, especially the poor rates (see table below)
- population changes and enclosure meant the poor were an increasingly visible presence in Elizabethan England
- changing economic circumstances, including problems with the wool trade, bad harvests and enclosure, forced the authorities (Crown, parliament and Justices of the Peace) to develop a more constructive attitude towards poverty.

To find out more about the effect of enclosures, go to page 28.

Elizabethans and poverty

Many Elizabethans distinguished between:

- the deserving or impotent poor (the old and the sick) who could not help themselves
- the idle poor (those who could work but chose not to do so).

It was felt the poor should be given every opportunity to better themselves. Those who refused to do so should be punished. Many Elizabethans remained suspicious of the poor and demonised them as counterfeits and criminals. Vagrants and vagabonds who deceived or threatened the public were dealt with severely: they could be whipped, imprisoned, enslaved or even hanged if caught begging.

Policies towards the poor in Elizabethan times

Action	Type of change	Detail
Poor rate	**Continuity** – these measures existed before Elizabeth's reign and continued throughout Tudor times.	A local tax organised by Justices of the Peace (JPs), with the proceeds spent on improving the lives of the poor. The poor were given money or things to make and sell.
Charity		Often funded by local wealthy people, who gave their name to the charitable foundation – e.g. Lady Cecil's Bequest for Poor Tradesmen, Romford.
Statute of Artificers, 1563	**Progressive** – government's response to increased unemployment caused by falls in the wool trade.	Those refusing to pay the poor rates could be put in prison. Officials who failed to organise poor relief could pay a penalty of up to £20.
1576 Poor Relief Act		JPs were required to provide the poor with wool and raw materials, to enable them to make and sell things. The poor who refused to do so were sent to a special prison known as the house of correction.
1572 Vagabonds Act	**Repressive** change that targeted vagrants. Parliament felt vagrants posed a threat to public order and had to be deterred through harsh punishment. Yet the Act also recognised the need to help the poor by providing them with work.	Vagrants were: • whipped and a hole drilled through each ear as a mark of shame, to warn others of their vagrancy • imprisoned if arrested again for vagrancy • given the death penalty for a third offence. The Act introduced a national poor rate, to provide support, including money and work, for the impotent poor. Justices of the Peace had to keep a register of the poor. Those in authority (JPs, parish councils, etc.) were tasked with finding work for the able bodied poor.

Now try this

Explain **two** ways in which the authorities in Elizabethan England tried to deal with poverty.

Factors promoting exploration

During Elizabeth's reign, English sailors and traders began to explore and develop trading links across the globe.

Expanding trade
- Trade was expanding quickly in the New World.
- English merchants needed new trading opportunities, as war with Spain and in the Netherlands had severely damaged the wool and cloth trades.
- It was vital to find new markets and new products to sell.

Adventure
- Some young Elizabethan men, such as Francis Drake, undertook voyages of discovery and exploration.
- The published accounts of these voyages, though often inaccurate, persuaded others to venture into the unknown in the belief that treasure and riches could be found and fortunes made.

Private investment
- Private investors, including Elizabeth I and her courtiers, funded many of the voyages of discovery.
- Although it was risky, the rewards could be enormous.
- This increased the incomes of both the Crown and the nobility.

New technology
Navigation was becoming increasingly more precise. The development of nautical devices, such as quadrants and astrolabes, made voyages safer, direct and faster, leading to more exploration and trade.

Reasons for exploration during the Elizabethan Age

The development of standardised maps, such as the Mercator Map of 1569, gave sailors and traders greater confidence that they were going in the right direction, reducing risk and encouraging further voyages.

Improvements in ship design
- Ships or galleons had bigger sails, were faster and more manoeuvrable, as well as possessing greater firepower to protect themselves from attack by pirates.
- They also were more stable and could take on more supplies, encouraging longer voyages and exploration.

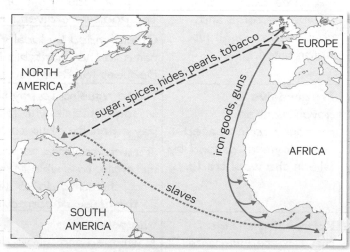

The triangular trade between West Africa, the New World and Europe.

The triangular trade
- The trader and explorer John Hawkins discovered that iron goods and guns could be sold in West Africa to buy slaves, which could be sold in the New World in exchange for rum, spices and tobacco, which would then be sold in Europe.
- Other merchants and traders across England copied this lucrative triangular trade.

Now try this

Explain **one** reason why voyages of exploration and discovery took place in Elizabethan times.

Drake's circumnavigation of the globe

Drake's circumnavigation of the globe took place between December 1577 and September 1580, after which the queen knighted him.

Why did Drake circumnavigate the globe?

- **He was attacking Spain.** Drake did not aim to sail around the world. His main purpose was to raid Spanish colonies in the Pacific, as relations with Spain were declining at this time.

- **Revenge.** The Spanish had attacked Drake's fleet at St Juan de Ulúa and most of his men had been killed.

- **Profit.** Loot, booty and trade meant there were huge profits to be made from Drake's proposed journey to the Americas and beyond, so people were willing to invest in the expedition, including Elizabeth I.

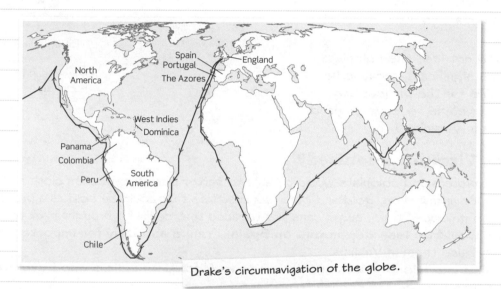

Drake's circumnavigation of the globe.

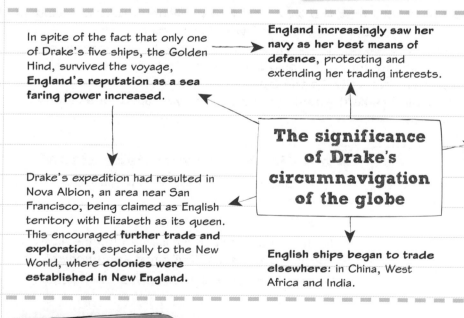

In spite of the fact that only one of Drake's five ships, the Golden Hind, survived the voyage, **England's reputation as a sea faring power increased.**

Drake's expedition had resulted in Nova Albion, an area near San Francisco, being claimed as English territory with Elizabeth as its queen. This encouraged **further trade and exploration**, especially to the New World, where **colonies were established in New England.**

England increasingly saw her navy as her best means of defence, protecting and extending her trading interests.

The significance of Drake's circumnavigation of the globe

English ships began to trade **elsewhere**: in China, West Africa and India.

Declining relations with Spain. Drake's voyage meant that England claimed the right to rule much of North America. This brought England into conflict with the pope, who had awarded North America to Spain, and with Spain itself, which had already conquered Mexico and Peru, and had established trading posts along the Eastern Pacific coast. For Philip II, the knighting of Drake on the Golden Hind by Elizabeth I was the final insult that made war between the two countries inevitable.

Now try this

Explain **two** consequences of Drake's circumnavigation of the globe.

Raleigh and the attempted colonisation of Virginia

In 1584–85, Sir Walter Raleigh organised, but did not participate in, a failed expedition to colonise Virginia on the east coast of North America.

Sir Walter Raleigh

- A noblemen and a courtier, he became an explorer during Elizabeth's reign.
- In 1584, Elizabeth gave Raleigh a grant to explore and settle lands in North America.
- Raleigh needed to raise huge amounts of money and encourage potential English colonists to leave their homes and settle in a land many knew little about.
- Raleigh did not lead the colonists, but he was significant because he raised funds for the project and persuaded people to leave England and settle in Virginia.

Timeline

The colonisation of Virginia

1585 English colonisation of Virginia begins; 107 men set out for Roanoke, Virginia.

1587 New English colonists return to Virginia and set up a colony at Roanoke.

1584 Raleigh plans new colonisation of North America and sends a team to explore Virginia and report back to him.

1586 The surviving colonists abandon the colony, after struggling to feed themselves and facing hostile Indians (Native Americans), and go back to England.

1590 English sailors arrive at Roanoke and discover that it has been abandoned and all of its colonists have disappeared.

Why was Virginia colonised?

1. **Trade.** Explorers and colonists would be able to barter ironware, woollen cloth and hunting knives in return for animal skins, gold and other commodities that could be sold at a profit. The colony could also produce crops, sugar cane and tobacco that could be brought back to England.
2. **England would be less dependent on Spain, France and Italy for imported goods** if it could produce them in Virginia.
3. **Welcoming and friendly natives**, including two Algonquian Indians who travelled back to England, encouraged the English to go there.
4. **Raleigh was able to persuade investors that the trip would be profitable.** People, including members of the nobility and the gentry, were prepared to invest in the expedition.
5. **Colonising Virginia would provide a base to attack Spanish settlements and colonies.** This would provide considerable loot and booty. It would also demonstrate to the Indian tribes that the English were a better alternative to the Spanish as rulers.
6. **A successful colony in Virginia would make it easier to fund other ventures**, opening up the New World to English settlement.

Who went to Virginia?

Raleigh did not lead the expedition, but a party of 107 colonists, almost all men, did set out for Roanoke, Virginia in 1585. The group, led by Richard Grenville, was mostly made up of soldiers and sailors, although there were some craftsmen, landowners, merchants and farmers.

What did the colonists take along?

- Food, and salt for preserving it – for the voyage and afterwards.
- Fresh water – for the voyage.
- Tools and equipment, including ploughs and seeds – to farm and build forts and homes.
- Weapons to protect themselves from attack.

Now try this

Explain **one** reason why Raleigh attempted to colonise Virginia in the 1580s.

The failure of Virginia

The Virginia colony failed for a range of different reasons.

Reasons why the colonisation of Virginia failed

Reason	Description	How it led to the failure of the colony
Lack of food	• First colonists left England too late to reach Virginia in time to plant crops. • One of their five ships let in seawater, ruining the food it was carrying.	• Unable to provide for themselves, those participating in the first expedition simply abandoned the colony in 1586. • The second "lost" colony may also have struggled to feed itself, making the colonists dependent on local Indian tribes.
Poor leadership	• The leader of the first expedition, Richard Grenville, was hot headed and did not get on with Ralph Lane, governor of the colony. • The leader of the second expedition, John White, abandoned the colony in 1587.	• Poor leadership meant that those involved in both expeditions had little direction or purpose. • This may explain the subsequent decision to abandon the first colony in 1586, as well as the fact that the second colony was found abandoned in 1590.
Lack of skills and experience	• Both expeditions lacked the experience and skill sets needed to make the expedition a success. • This meant both expeditions were doomed from the start.	• Merchants and landowners lacked physical capacity for manual work. • A lack of stonemasons meant that a stone fort was never built, leaving the colony vulnerable to Indian attack. • Soldiers could defend the expedition but lacked the ability to farm the land.
Native American attack	• In 1586, angered by the diseases they had brought, Algonquian Chief Winginia led an attack on the colonists. • Other Indian tribes, suspicious of the English and angered by their demands for food, also attacked between 1585 and 1586.	• Winginia's attack was beaten off but led to a crisis within the first expedition, forcing the colonists to abandon Roanoke. • It is possible a second expedition was wiped out by an Indian attack led by Chief Powhatan. • Alternatively, an attack may have led to some of the settlers becoming slaves or being assimilated into local Indian tribes.
The war with Spain	• From 1585, England was effectively at war with Spain.	• The threat from the Armada meant that few ships were available to visit or resupply the colonists. • The colonists were increasingly isolated and vulnerable to attack.

The significance of the attempted colonisation of Virginia

The colony was a failure but it did serve as a template for future settlements, including that at Jamestown in 1607.

By the end of the 17th century, 13 colonies, each with their own system of government, had been established along the eastern seaboard of the New World.

Now try this

Explain **one** reason why the attempt to colonise Virginia failed between 1587 and 1590.

Exam overview

This page introduces you to the main features and requirements of the Paper 2 Option B4 exam paper.

About Paper 2

- Paper 2 is for both your period study and your British depth study.
- Early Elizabethan England is a British depth study – it will be in Section B of Paper 2: Tudor depth options.
- Early Elizabethan England is Option B4. You will see where it starts on the exam paper with a heading like this:

> The Paper 2 exam lasts for 1 hour 45 minutes (105 minutes) in total. There are 32 marks for the period study and 32 marks for this depth study, so you should spend about 50 minutes on each.

> **Option B4: Early Elizabethan England, 1558–88**

> Remember to read each question carefully before you start to answer it.

The three questions

The three questions for Option B4 will always follow this pattern.

Question 4(a)

Describe **two features of …**   **(4 marks)**

> This question targets Assessment Objective 1 (AO1): it focuses on describing features.

> Assessment Objective 1 (AO1) is where you show your knowledge and understanding of the key features and characteristics of Early Elizabethan England 1558–1588.

> You can see examples of all three questions on pages 35–40 of this Skills section, and in the Practice section on pages 41–52.

Question 4(b)

Explain why …   **(12 marks)**

Two prompts and your own information

> This question targets both AO1 and AO2. It focuses on causation: explaining why something happened.

Question 4(c)

Choice of two questions: **(16 marks)**
(c)(i) or (c)(ii)

[Statement] and How far do you agree? Explain your answer.

Two prompts and your own information

> You have a choice of two questions. These target both AO1 and AO2. You need to make a judgement in this question.

> Assessment Objective 2 (AO2) is where you explain and analyse key events using historical concepts such as causation, consequence, change, continuity, similarity, difference.

Question 5(a): Describing features 1

Question 5(a) on your exam paper will ask you to 'Describe **two** features of...'. There are four marks available for this question: two for each feature you describe.

Worked example

Describe **two** features of the Ridolfi plot.

(4 marks)

 Links You can revise the Ridolfi plot on page 16.

What is a feature?
A **feature** is something that is distinctive or characteristic. For example, we can tell one person from another because of their distinctive facial features. So, when a question asks for two features of something, think about the special characteristics of that something.

Sample answer

Make sure you have sufficient detail here, as this answer needs more supporting information.

Feature 1
The Ridolfi plot was an attempt to murder Elizabeth I and replace her with Mary, Queen of Scots.

Feature 2
The plot failed and the conspirators were executed.

Remember to look at two different aspects of the plot: what it planned to do, and its failure or its significance.

Improved answer

Feature 1
The Ridolfi plot took place in 1571. It was an attempt to murder Elizabeth I and replace her with Mary, Queen of Scots. The plot was organised by Roberto Ridolfi, an Italian banker and one of the pope's spies. Once Elizabeth was murdered, a Spanish invasion would take place and Mary would then be married to the Duke of Norfolk.

The student has correctly identified a feature of the Ridolfi plot (what the plotters planned to do) and has added good supporting information.

Feature 2
William Cecil uncovered the plot and, in 1571, proved that the Duke of Norfolk had plotted against Elizabeth. In May 1572, parliament demanded Norfolk's execution and he was beheaded the following month.

The student has identified another feature of the Ridolfi plot: its failure. Relevant detail has been added, showing how the plot failed and the fate of the plotters.

Question 5(a): Describing features 2

Question 5(a) on your exam paper will ask you to 'Describe **two** features of...'. There are four marks available for this question: two for each feature you describe.

 You can revise Elizabethan Society on page 2.

What does 'describe' mean?
Describe means to give an account of the main characteristics of something.

 Worked example

Describe **two** features of Elizabethan society.

(4 marks)

Remember: you develop your description with relevant details, but you do not need to include reasons or justifications.

Sample answer

Feature 1

There was a social hierarchy in the countryside.

 This is a correct feature of English society, but the answer is rather vague and does not demonstrate enough knowledge.

Feature 2

In the towns there were craftsmen, merchants and unskilled labourers.

 This answer describes aspects of English society but it needs to be refocused so that it describes a feature: a special characteristic of English society.

 The student has included some specific detail here – craftsmen, merchants and unskilled labourers – but more support is needed to back up the student's description.

Improved answer

Feature 1

There was a social hierarchy in the countryside. At the top were the nobility and the gentry. Below them were the yeomen farmers and tenant farmers (who often rented land from the nobility and gentry) as well as the landless and labouring poor.

 The student has added details that support the key feature: the social hierarchy in the countryside.

Feature 2

There was also a social hierarchy in the towns. At the top were the merchants (who traded in goods). Below them were the professionals (doctors and lawyers), business owners, craftsmen (skilled labourers or artisans), unskilled labourers and the unemployed.

 This answer has now been refocused and describes the features of Elizabethan society in the towns and cities.

Question 5(b): Explaining why 1

Question 5(b) on your exam paper is about causation: explaining why something happened. There are 12 marks available for this question and two prompts to help you answer it. You must also use information of your own.

Worked example

Explain why the revolt of the Northern Earls took place in 1569.   **(12 marks)**

You may use the following in your answer:
- Mary, Queen of Scots
- Catholicism.

You **must** also use information of your own.

What does 'explain' mean?

Explain means saying how or why something happened, backed up with examples or justifications to support the reasons you give.

A good way to get into an explanation is to use sentence starters, such as 'One reason for this was...', or 'This was because...'.

Sample answer

 You can revise the reasons for the Revolt of the Northern Earls on page 15.

The Revolt of the Northern Earls took place because many Catholics did not want to be ruled by a Protestant monarch. This was especially the case in the north of England, where both the nobility and the population remained Catholic.

 The first sentence of the answer is very strong. It relates directly to the question and sets up a clear line of argument but does not develop it.

The northern nobility, including the Percys and the Nevilles, did not like the way that Elizabeth had promoted new favourites within the court and the Privy Council, such as William Cecil and Robert Dudley.

 The second paragraph demonstrates good factual knowledge (AO1), but does not explain why the northern nobility's resentment of Elizabeth's favourites boiled over into open rebellion (AO2). This section should be **explaining** why the Northern Earls' resentment led to open rebellion.

The Northern Earls believed that if Elizabeth were to be replaced by Mary, Queen of Scots, then Catholicism would be restored in England and the power of the Northern Earls would be restored. Mary, Queen of Scots, Elizabeth's second cousin, had fled Scotland in 1568 and was now imprisoned in England. She also had a claim to the throne and was Catholic.

 The third paragraph picks up the other prompt of the question: Mary, Queen of Scots. Again, the student demonstrates good factual knowledge but there is only one point at which they give any explanation: 'Catholicism would be restored in England and the power of the Northern Earls would be restored.' The factual information at the end of the paragraph is good but is not used to support the explanation.

Compare this answer with an improved version on the next page.

Question 5(b): Explaining why 2

This page has more details about answering a Question 5(b) question, and an improved version of the answer given on the previous page.

Improved answer

The Revolt of the Northern Earls took place for a number of reasons, including Catholic anger, the resentment of the northern nobility and the chance to put Mary, Queen of Scots, on the throne.

Northern England remained an area where Catholicism had endured in England. Many Catholics resented Elizabeth's religious settlement, as well as her appointment of the arch Protestant James Pilkington as Bishop of Durham. A revolt would allow Catholicism to be restored and with it the Catholic liturgy and religious calendar.

Linked to this was the seething resentment of the northern nobility. The Northern Earls, such as the Percys and the Nevilles, had always enjoyed independence from the Crown as to how the north was administered and governed, and influence at court and on the Privy Council. They disliked Elizabeth's new favourites at court, including William Cecil and Robert Dudley, who were Protestants and lacked the status of the Northern Earls. A revolt, if successful, would remove the new influences at court and allow the influence of traditional northern families to be restored.

Finally, the arrival of Mary, Queen of Scots, in England in 1568 strengthened the Northern Earls' willingness to revolt. Mary, a Catholic, was Elizabeth's second cousin and had a claim to the English throne. Removing Elizabeth and replacing her with Mary as queen would allow Catholicism and the influence of the northern nobility at court to be restored.

Causation questions

Question 5(b) is about causation – causes. These questions have:

- 6 marks for AO1 (accurate and relevant information)

- 6 marks for AO2 (explanation and analysis). Strong answers combine explanation and analysis (AO2) with relevant information (AO1).

Use your first paragraph to signpost your answer and show the direction in which it is going.

Ensure your second paragraph focuses on explaining **why** the resentment of Catholics led to the revolt. AO1 detail (accurate and relevant information) is required and should now be used to support the explanation (AO2)

The third paragraph also now has a focus on **explaining how** the resentment of the northern nobility led directly to revolt against Elizabeth.

In the final paragraph, use your own knowledge to show how the arrival of Mary, Queen of Scots, offered an alternative monarchy to that of Elizabeth and led to the Northern Revolt. Here, the answer attempts to link this point with the points made in the previous two paragraphs.

Analysis is about examining something carefully in order to identify the reasons that explain it. The most successful answers to 5(b) questions provide an **analytical explanation**. This means you must focus on what the question is asking, and select reasons that provide an explanation that has been thought through carefully.

This is an improved version of the answer on the previous page.

Question 5(c): Making a judgement 1

Question 5(c) on your exam paper involves analysing the statement in the question and deciding how far you agree with it. There are 16 marks available for this question and two prompts to help you answer. You must also use information of your own.

Worked example

'Religion was the main cause of the growing tension between England and Spain between 1570 and 1588.' How far do you agree? Explain your answer. **(16 marks)**

You may use the following in your answer:

- the pope's excommunication of Elizabeth
- the Dutch revolt.

You **must** also use information of your own.

Sample answer

Religion was a reason why relations between England and Spain deteriorated between 1570 and 1588. England remained a Protestant country and saw the papacy and Catholic Spain as a threat. Catholic Spain saw Protestantism as something that had to be stamped out, so the pope excommunicated Elizabeth and encouraged Philip II to plot against her.

The Dutch revolt was also an important reason why relations broke down. Many Dutchmen were Protestants and did not want to be ruled by Spain. The Duke of Alba treated Dutch Protestants very badly, while the Spanish Fury took place in Antwerp in 1580. This angered many English Protestants.

Finally there was also English privateering. English sailors, including Drake, attacked Spanish ships and raided Spanish colonies in Latin America. This angered Spain, as its wealth was significantly reduced by these attacks.

Religion was always the main reason why relations between England and Spain got worse between 1570 and 1588, although other reasons, including the Dutch Revolt and English privateering, were also important.

Compare this answer with an improved version on the next page.

Analysing the statement

The statement in question 5(c) will start by referring to '...the main cause of...' or 'The main reason for...'. You decide whether you agree or not by considering whether other reasons were more important.

Remember: you need to make a judgement when answering question 5(c).

 Links You can revise relations with Spain on pages 20–21 and the war with Spain on pages 22–25.

You have a choice of two questions for question 5(c).

 The first paragraph starts well and links religion to relations between England and Spain. You need to provide sufficient detail, or show how religious differences led to increased hostility.

 The second paragraph is undeveloped and does not link to the question. You need to show how the Dutch revolt brought Britain and Spain to the brink of war.

 Like the second paragraph, this is mostly descriptive and not **analytical**. You need to explain why privateering led to declining relations with Spain, as one of a number of reasons why relations with Spain deteriorated between 1570 and 1588.

 It is not until the conclusion that the student fully addresses the question and compares the different reasons involved. When summarising, you need to ensure the evidence you include is detailed enough.

Question 5(c): Making a judgement 2

This page has more details about answering a Question 5(c) question and has an improved version of the answer on the previous page.

Improved answer

Religion was a major cause of the growing tension between England and Spain, but other factors were also important, including the Dutch revolt, English piracy and Spain's involvement in plots against Elizabeth.

Religion underpinned the growing tension between Spain and England. England was a Protestant country and the key members of Elizabeth's Privy Council were all Protestant. Spain, under Philip II, remained Catholic with close links to the papacy. So, England increasingly saw Catholic Spain as a threat to the Protestant faith and queen, while Spain saw England as a country that needed to become Catholic again. These conflicting positions meant relations between England and Spain deteriorated in the 1570s.

This situation was made worse by Spain's involvement in the Ridolfi, Babington and Throckmorton plots against Elizabeth, which convinced Elizabeth's government that Spain, with troops in the Netherlands, posed a threat. Spain's involvement in the plots also proved that English Catholics could not be trusted. This led to tough measures against English Catholics (recusants) as well as the eventual execution of Mary, Queen of Scots. This in turn convinced Philip II that Catholicism in England could only be preserved through military action, including invasion.

The revolt in the Netherlands was also important. Events, such as the Council of Troubles and the Spanish Fury, convinced Elizabeth's government to provide assistance to the Protestant Dutch rebels. Spain saw this as unacceptable interference in the way it governed the Netherlands.

Piracy and privateering also played a role. English sailors had been raiding Spanish ships and colonies in the New World. When Elizabeth knighted Drake on the Golden Hind, this insulted the Spanish. Yet, Elizabeth's government resented Spanish control of Antwerp and the mouth of the Rhine, which made it harder for English merchants to export goods to Europe. So, there were commercial reasons for declining relations.

In conclusion, religion was a major factor in explaining England's deteriorating relationship with Spain, and this is linked to other factors, such as the Dutch revolt and the plots against Elizabeth. Yet there were also commercial reasons for the declining relationship.

The balance of Assessment Objectives

Question 5(c) is worth 16 marks in total:
- 6 marks are available for AO1
- 10 marks are available for AO2.

This shows the importance of analysis and explanation. AO1 information and understanding also needs to be combined with AO2 explanation and analysis for the best results.

You have a choice of two questions for question 5(c). Each 5(c) question targets both AO1 and AO2.

Links You can revise relations with Spain on pages 20–21 and the war with Spain on pages 22–25.

Remember to try to signpost your answer in the first paragraph.

Paragraphs 2 to 4 consider other factors. Compare them and try to link them together.

In your final paragraph, you should aim to compare the reasons and reach an overall judgement.

This is an improved version of the answer on the previous page.

Practice

Put your skills and knowledge into practice with the following question.

Option B4: Early Elizabethan England 1558–1588

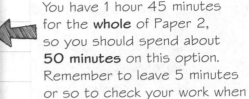
You have 1 hour 45 minutes for the **whole** of Paper 2, so you should spend about **50 minutes** on this option. Remember to leave 5 minutes or so to check your work when you've finished writing.

Answer Question 5(a), 5(b) and **EITHER** 5(c)(i) **OR** 5(c)(ii).

5 (a) Describe **two** features of Elizabeth's religious settlement of 1559.   **(4 marks)**

Links You can revise Elizabeth's religious settlement on page 8.

Feature 1

Guided One feature of the religious settlement was the

Act of Supremacy, 1559. This made

....

....

....

....

You need to identify **two** valid features and support each feature.

Feature 2

....

....

 An example of a suitable feature might be the Act of Supremacy, and a suitable supporting statement could be 'This made Elizabeth Supreme Governor of the Church of England'. (You could also mention the fact that all clergy had to swear allegiance to her as Head of the Church.)

....

....

....

....

 Your exam paper will have a separate space for each feature you need to describe.

 Describe means you have to give an account of the main characteristics of the feature. You do not need to explain why the feature was important, or what it was trying to achieve.

Practice

Put your skills and knowledge into practice with the following question.

5 (b) Explain why attempts to colonise Virginia in the 1580s failed. **(12 marks)**

You may use the following in your answer:
- lack of food
- Native American (Indian) attacks.

You must also use information of your own.

....

....

....

....

....

....

....

....

....

....

....

....

....

....

....

....

....

....

....

....

Remember that question 5(b) is all about **causation**: this means you are looking for relevant reasons. For example, you might refer to the fact that the settlers lacked food as one of the ships, the Tiger, had let in seawater; ruining the food it was carrying.

Links You can revise the failure of the Virginia settlement on page 33.

There are 12 marks on offer for this question. You don't have to use the prompts in the question in your answer, but you **must** include your own information to answer the question fully.

For this question you must give **at least two reasons**, even if they are all your own, and combine them to create a good explanation. The use of phrases, such as 'This led to', or 'This resulted in', will help you to do this.

Practice

Use this page to continue your answer to question 5(b).

....

....

....

....

....

....

....

....

....

....

....

....

....

....

....

....

....

....

....

....

....

....

....

....

....

....

....

Your explanations need to stay focused on answering the question. Although you might remember lots of detail about the Virginia colony, remember to focus on providing **reasons why it failed**, and not descriptions of what happened to it. For example, you might explain that the colonists were reduced to starvation because of a lack of food. This meant that they had to trade with the Native Americans for food. This meant that there was contact between the settlers and the Native Americans, allowing diseases to spread. This led to...

Remember: the best answers to Question 5(b) will:
• show a good knowledge of the key features and characteristics of the period
and:
• analyse causation, showing how factors combined to bring about an outcome.

Make sure you support your explanation with a good range of accurate and relevant detail throughout your answer.

Practice

Put your skills and knowledge into practice with the following question.

Answer EITHER 5(c)(i) OR 5(c)(ii).

EITHER

5 (c) (i) 'Religion was Elizabeth's main problem when she became queen of England in 1558.' How far do you agree? **(16 marks)**

    You may use the following in your answer:

      • Elizabeth's religious settlement of 1559

      • the Puritans.

    You **must** also use information of your own.

OR

5 (c) (ii) 'The main consequence of the Revolt of the Northern Earls in 1569 was the setting up of the Council of the North.' How far do you agree? Explain your answer. **(16 marks)**

    You may use the following in your answer:

      • the Council of the North

      • Mary, Queen of Scots.

    You **must** also use information of your own.

For **Question 5(c)**, you have a **choice of two questions**. Each question is worth the same number of marks. Although one might immediately seem a question you can answer, do read both carefully to check your choice is the right one.

On the exam paper, the two options for Question 5(c) will be on one page, and you will then turn to the next page to write your answer – like the layout here.

If you decide to answer question 5(c)(i), turn to page 45. If you decide to answer 4(c)(ii), turn to page 49.

Links You can revise the problems Elizabeth faced when she became queen on pages 1–6. For more about the Revolt of the Northern Earls, see pages 15–16.

Choosing a question

At the top of the first answer page there will be an instruction for you to indicate which of the two questions you have chosen to answer. You do this by making a cross in the box for 5(c)(i) or 5(c)(ii). (You can see this on pages 45 and 49.) Don't worry if you put a cross in the wrong box by mistake. Just put a line through the cross and then put a new cross in the correct box.

Practice

Put your skills and knowledge into practice with the following question.

Indicate which question you are answering by marking a cross in the box. If you change your mind, put a line through the box and then indicate your new question with a cross.

Chosen question: 5(c)(i) ☒ 5(c)(ii) ☐

Guided Religion was a major issue confronting Elizabeth on her accession to the throne in 1558 as the country was divided between Catholics and Protestants, making a religious settlement difficult. However, Elizabeth also faced other problems: her legitimacy as monarch was in doubt and she faced financial problems while she also faced threats from abroad in the form of Spain and France.

....

....

....

....

....

....

....

....

....

....

....

....

....

....

....

....

....

....

Plan your answer **before** you start writing. List factors that support the statement in the question, and list other factors that go against the statement.

For example:

Support	Against
Divided country	Legitimacy
Catholicism strong, especially in the north	Threats from other countries – Spain and France
Puritans	Financial problems
Religious settlement – an attempt at compromise	

Spending a couple of minutes planning your answer means you can write an introduction setting up your arguments. This signposts your answer, making it easier to write and understand.

For each point you make, always go on to explain how it relates to the question.

Practice

Use this page to continue your answer to question 5(c)(i).

Guided Religion was undoubtedly a problem facing

Elizabeth. England was a divided country in 1558.

Protestants were more numerous in the south of England,

especially in London. However, in the north of England

....

....

....

....

....

....

....

....

....

....

....

....

....

....

....

....

....

....

....

....

....

....

....

....

....

....

....

Remember **only** to answer **either** Question 5(c)(i) **or** Question 5(c)(ii) in the exam.

This paragraph is structured to address the question. It follows from the introductory paragraph on the previous page. Link all points back to the question.

As with question 5(b), you do not have to use both or either of the two prompts provided by the question. If you do use them, remember that you **must** also include information of your own.

End your answer by saying **how far** you agree with the question statement, and provide support for your decision. Try to weigh the evidence and compare the problems Elizabeth faced in 1558.

For example, you might conclude that religion was important because England was divided and the loyalty of Catholics and Puritans remained in doubt. However, other factors remained important: Crown finances were in a mess, Elizabeth's legitimacy remained in doubt, and she faced threats from Spain and France.

Practice

Use this page to continue your answer to question 5(c)(i).

Practice

Use this page to continue your answer to question 5(c)(i).

Practice

Put your skills and knowledge into practice with the following question.

Indicate which question you are answering by marking a cross in the box. If you change your mind, put a line through the box and then indicate your new question with a cross.

Chosen question: 5(c)(i) ☐   5(c)(ii) ☒

Remember: Question 5(c) gives you a choice of two questions. **In the exam, you only need to answer either 5(c)(i) or 5(c)(ii).**

Guided The Council of the North was a major consequence of the Revolt of the Northern Earls. However, the revolt also brought into focus the potential disloyalty of Catholics, as well as the fact that Mary, Queen of Scots, as an alternative monarch, could encourage further revolts.

This question asks about **consequences**: 'The main consequence of the revolt of the Northern Earls in 1569 was the setting up of the Council of the North.' Consequences are the **results** of something. Be careful not to write about 'reasons for' instead of 'results of'.

Remember: it is a good idea to signpost your answer to the question, so that the points you raise can be developed over the course of your answer.

Write in short paragraphs and link each point you make back to the question.

For example, you might state that the revolt had shown that the north of England remained dangerously beyond Elizabeth's control. This led to the setting up of the Council of the North, which sought to reimpose Elizabeth's authority within the region.

Practice

Use this page to continue your answer to question 5(c)(ii).

....
....
....
....
....
....
....
....
....
....
....
....
....
....
....
....
....
....
....
....
....
....
....
....
....

As with Question 5(b), you do not have to use both or either of the two prompts provided by the question. If you do use them, remember that you **must** also include information of your own.

Bring specific facts and details into your answer to show how well you understand the key features and characteristics that are involved in the question.

When you end your answer, make sure you say **how far** you agree with the question statement and provide support for your decision.

Practice

Use this page to continue your answer to question 5(c)(ii).

Practice

Use this page to continue your answer to question 5(c)(ii).

Answers

Where an example answer is given, this is not necessarily the only correct response. In most cases there is a range of responses that can gain full marks.

SUBJECT CONTENT

Queen, government and religion, 1558–69

England in 1558

1. Government on Elizabeth's accession

1 One key feature of Elizabethan government was the court. Courtiers tended to be members of the nobility who acted as the monarch's advisers and friends. The court's principal role was to entertain, advise and influence the monarch as well as display the monarch's wealth and power.

Another key feature of Elizabethan government was the Privy Council. This was made up of members of the nobility, courtiers and advisers. It met three times a week and was often presided over by the monarch. It dealt with issues in government policy, carried out government decisions, monitored the Justices of the Peace and parliament, and oversaw law and order and the security of the country.

2 Elizabeth's powers were limited by parliament. The queen could rule by decree to protect the country in time of war and was, from 1559, Head of the Church of England. However, she could only pass laws with parliament's consent (these were known as Acts of Parliament) while she required parliament's permission if she wished to raise additional taxes. This was known as extraordinary taxation. Elizabeth could, of course, refuse to summon parliament, and could even try to bribe or intimidate individual MPs or members of the House of Lords. However, ignoring parliament threatened her popularity and damaged her authority as monarch.

2. Society on Elizabeth's accession

Answers can refer to any of the following points:

- There was a predefined social hierarchy in which everyone 'knew their place'. In the countryside, this involved the nobility (landowners) at the top, followed by the gentry, yeomen and tenant farmers, and finally the landless labourers. In the towns, the merchants dominated, followed by professionals (lawyers, physicians), craftsmen and labourers.
- There was a tradition of **obedience and care** wherever you were in Elizabethan society. You owed respect and obedience to those above you, and a duty of care to those below you. Landowners ran their estates on this basis. This meant that they were obliged to take care of their tenants, especially in times of hardship.
- There were few opportunities for social mobility. People in the countryside could not climb the social ladder by becoming members of the gentry or major landowners. Instead, they were expected to remain in the social group into which they were born. In the towns, there were more opportunities for personal advancement. The emergence of grammar schools meant that people could improve their position in society by becoming physicians or doctors, for example.

3. Virgin Queen: legitimacy, gender and marriage

Answers can refer to any two of the following points:

- Gender – Elizabeth was female and it was unusual for a queen to rule in her own right. Many people disapproved of the idea of a queen regnant, a female ruler with the power to make decisions rather than simply being a figurehead (a ruler without real power).
- Legitimacy – Elizabeth was the daughter of Anne Boleyn, who Henry VIII had married after divorcing Catherine of Aragon. The pope had refused to recognise Anne's marriage to Henry VIII and therefore regarded Elizabeth, her daughter, as having an illegitimate claim to the English throne.
- Elizabeth was only 21 years old and inexperienced. She needed the support of her Privy Council and her Secretary of State, William Cecil.
- The Crown was £300 000 in debt and the queen needed to raise additional money. However doing so would be unpopular and require the support of parliament.

4. Virgin Queen: character and strengths

Answers can refer to any two of the following advantages:

- Elizabeth was confident and charismatic – this enabled her to win over her subjects and command support in parliament.
- Elizabeth was resilient – she had spent time in the Tower accused of treason and facing possible execution. She could cope with the pressures of being queen.
- Although Elizabeth was Protestant, the number of Protestants in England was growing, making her position as queen more secure. She could claim divine right with growing conviction.
- Elizabeth had an excellent grasp of politics – she understood the interests and ambitions of her subjects, and was able to use her powers of patronage effectively. This meant that she could reward her supporters by giving them lucrative positions in local government, such as Justice of the Peace or Lord Lieutenant.
- Elizabeth was well educated – she spoke Latin, Greek, French and Italian. This made it more difficult to conceal information from the queen. Latin and French remained the language of diplomacy in the 16th century, and Elizabeth was able to use this to her advantage.

5. Challenges at home: financial weaknesses

Elizabeth faced many financial problems because a series of costly wars had left England heavily in debt. Moreover, under her predecessor Mary Tudor, costly wars meant Crown lands were sold off, making England even more heavily in debt and increasing Elizabeth's dependence on parliament. Therefore, Crown revenues were falling at a time when Crown expenditure, especially on warfare, had increased. By 1558, the Crown was £300 000 in debt, of which £100 000 was owed to foreign moneylenders – the Antwerp Exchange – who charged interest at 14%. Crown revenues, meanwhile, had fallen to £286 667. This made Elizabeth increasingly dependent on parliament for money, as parliament would have to approve additional taxes or subsidies. Increasing taxes would make Elizabeth unpopular with major landowners, members of the gentry and merchants at a time when she faced considerable opposition, not least among Catholics. The alternative, debasing the currency by reducing its silver, would only cause a rise in inflation.

6. Challenges abroad: France, Scotland and Spain

Elizabeth faced challenges from France, Scotland and potentially Spain when she became queen in 1558.

France and England had been at war during Mary's reign, resulting in the loss of Calais at the Treaty of Cateau-Cambrésis (1559). However, France remained a dangerous enemy, as it had a larger population than England. More importantly, the 'Auld Alliance' between France and Scotland meant that Elizabeth potentially faced war with both countries at the same time.

The threat from France was reduced by its war with Spain. However, the end of the conflict meant that both France and Spain, the main Catholic kingdoms in Europe, could threaten Protestant England. This threat was made worse by the fact that Elizabeth's cousin, Mary, Queen of Scots, was married to Francis II, so France could attack England to support Mary's claim to the English throne.

The religious settlement

7. Religious divisions in England in 1558

Key ways in which the beliefs of Catholics, Protestants and Puritans differed in 1558 include:

- Church offices: Catholics argued that there was need for a pope as well as cardinals and bishops. Mainstream Protestants argued there was no need for a pope (the monarch under the Act of Supremacy replaced him), but that there remained a need for bishops. Puritans took an entirely different position, arguing that all clerical offices including bishops were unnecessary.
- Style of service: Catholics required highly decorated churches containing candles, statues and other religious icons. Protestants wanted a simpler style of worship with fewer decorations and icons. Puritans saw all church decorations as a distraction and argued that they should be removed.
- Catholics required their clergy to wear coloured vestments. Mainstream Protestants required simple vestments, while Puritans saw vestments as completely unnecessary.

8. Elizabeth's religious settlement

1 Any two of the following explanations are valid:
- The Act of Supremacy, 1559 – made Elizabeth Supreme Governor of the Church of England: all clergy and officials had to swear an oath of allegiance to her.
- The Act of Uniformity, 1559 – shaped the appearance of English churches and the forms of services they held.
- The Royal Injunctions, 1559 – this was a set of instructions to the clergy on a wide range of issues. The Injunctions reinforced the Acts of Supremacy and Uniformity and included information on how people should worship God and the structure of church services.
- The Book of Common Prayer had to be used in all church services.
- An Ecclesiastical High Commission was introduced, to maintain discipline within the Church and enforce the queen's religious settlement.

2 Answers should refer to two of the following reasons:
- Protestants would have approved of the new communion sacrament referred to in the Book of Common Prayer. They would have interpreted this as an Act of Remembrance that did not involve transubstantiation.
- Protestants would also have approved of Elizabeth's willingness to assert her authority over the Church. Under Mary Tudor, the pope had asserted his rule as Head of the English Church. Through the Act of Supremacy and the Ecclesiastical High Commission, Elizabeth and not the pope was Head of the English Church.
- Protestant support for this settlement would have been reinforced by the removal of the Marian Bishops, who had opposed the religious settlement of 1559.
- Protestants would have approved of the ban on pilgrimages and 'fake miracles', which they would have seen as Catholic practices.
- Protestants would have approved of the Book of Common Prayer, which asserted that all church services had to be in English rather than Latin (the language commonly used in the Catholic Mass).

9. Church of England: its role in society

1 The Church of England controlled English society in a number of ways:
- It controlled what was preached, as clergy required a special licence to preach. Clergy who did not conform to the religious settlement or show support for the queen lost their licence to preach.

- It enforced the Religious Settlement of 1559.
- It gave guidance to communities, especially during times of hardship and uncertainty.
- It ran the Church Courts, dealing with marriages, sexual offences, wills and slander.
- It legitimised the power of the monarch and encouraged people to stay loyal to the queen.

2 The clergy played a key role in rural parishes. They provided both spiritual and practical guidance to ordinary people. Spiritual guidance involved church services as well as marriages, baptisms and funerals. Practical guidance involved providing support for parishioners, especially in times of crisis, including bad harvests. The clergy also played an educational role through parish schools.

The clergy were also responsible for the enforcement of Elizabeth's religious settlement. They monitored church attendance while ensuring that church services conformed to the Book of Common Prayer. By their preaching they were required to encourage loyalty to the queen as Head of the Church of England, as well as to local members of the gentry who endowed (funded) churches.

The clergy were also required on occasion to appear before the Church Courts relating to matters affecting their parish. These could include marriages, sexual offences, wills and slander.

Religious challenges
10. The Puritan challenge

Puritans challenged the English Church over vestments and crucifixes. Under the religious settlement of 1559 Elizabeth was happy to place a crucifix in all English churches. Puritans challenged this, arguing that this was a Catholic symbol and that churches should not contain religious icons and ornaments.

Under the religious settlement of 1559, clergy were required to wear special vestments. Puritans challenged this, arguing that clergy should either wear no vestments or simple vestments.

11. The Catholic challenge at home

Catholics opposed Elizabeth's religious settlement for a number of reasons:
- Many Catholics disliked the Protestant tone of Elizabeth's religious settlement of 1559, especially the end of Holy Days, pilgrimages and the use of religious icons.
- Many Catholics remained uncomfortable with the style of worship required by the Book of Common Prayer, which gave services a Protestant tone, as the number of sacraments were reduced while the service, no longer strictly a mass, was said in English rather than Latin.
- Other Catholics disliked the fact that priests could now marry and no longer wore coloured vestments in religious services.
- Many Catholics also objected to the Act of Supremacy, which made Queen Elizabeth and not the pope Head of the Church of England. Indeed, the pope's requirement in 1566 that Catholics no longer attend Church of England services further reinforced opposition to the settlement.

12. The Catholic challenge abroad

Relations between Spain and England declined in the following ways between 1560 and 1570:
- Spanish rule in the Netherlands, especially the Council of Troubles, resulted in hundreds of Dutch Protestants being put to death. This alarmed many Protestants on Elizabeth's Privy Council, including William Cecil. They felt that Spain's actions demonstrated that Spain remained a very real threat to the Protestant faith, both in Europe and in England. This was because Spanish troops across the English Channel in the Spanish Netherlands were now ideally placed to invade England.
- The English seizure of the Genoese loan in 1568 from Spanish ships that were sheltering in English ports angered Spain, who viewed the action as an act of piracy directed against Spanish property.
- Finally, the excommunication of Elizabeth in 1570 encouraged Catholic powers to view attacking England as a means of installing a Catholic monarch on the throne.

Mary, Queen of Scots
13. Mary's claim to the throne and arrival in England

Mary was imprisoned for a range of different reasons. She had a valid claim to the throne and could incite rebellion against Elizabeth, especially in the north of England where loyalty to the Catholic cause remained strong and she could win the support of the Northern Earls. Imprisoning Mary, and restricting access to her, would reduce her political influence within the country and the threat she posed to Elizabeth.
There was also the danger that Mary could return to France and revive the 'Auld Alliance' between France and Scotland as a means of regaining her throne. This would threaten English security. Imprisoning Mary would, by keeping Mary in England, prevent this from happening. Finally Elizabeth could not execute Mary as this would anger France and Spain and weaken Elizabeth's authority as she would have executed an anointed monarch. Keeping Mary in comfortable captivity meant that Elizabeth could reduce the danger to herself.

14. Mary vs Elizabeth

Mary posed a threat to Elizabeth because she had a claim to the throne as her second cousin. Moreover, unlike Elizabeth, there was no questioning her legitimacy, as Mary was descended from Henry VII. Elizabeth, on the other hand, was descended from Anne Boleyn, who was subsequently executed by her father, Henry VIII. This cast doubt on Elizabeth's claim to the throne, further adding to the threat posed by Mary as an alternative monarch.

Mary had been married to Francis II of France and there was always the possibility that France might seek to support Mary's claim to the throne. Moreover, English Catholics saw Mary, a Catholic, as an alternative monarch to Elizabeth and they were therefore more likely to risk rebellion in order to place Mary on the throne. The pope's decision in 1570 to excommunicate Elizabeth heightened this threat, as it meant that Catholics were obliged to act against Elizabeth and support Mary's claim to the throne.

Other foreign powers, including Spain, were also prepared to engage in plots and conspiracies that would depose Protestant Queen Elizabeth and put Catholic Queen Mary on the throne.

Challenges to Elizabeth at home and abroad, 1569–88

Plots and revolts at home

15. The Revolt of the Northern Earls

1 The Revolt of the Northern Earls threatened Elizabeth's position as monarch for a number of reasons. First, it demonstrated that the loyalty of the nobility could not be taken for granted. Rather, members of the nobility, especially those with family connections, including the Nevilles, the Percys and the Duke of Norfolk, were capable of plotting against monarchs to advance themselves socially and politically. It also showed how members of the nobility, whose influence at court had been reduced, were capable of plotting against the queen. Moreover, it demonstrated the disloyalty of the queen's Catholic subjects. They opposed Elizabeth's religious settlement of 1559, especially the end of the Latin mass, pilgrimages and Holy Days. They also disliked attempts by James Pilkington, an arch Protestant appointed Bishop of Durham, to impose the settlement on the North of England. The revolt showed how many Catholics were able to engage in plots and conspiracies to depose Elizabeth and restore Catholicism to England.

The revolt also demonstrated the threat posed by Mary, Queen of Scots. It had provided the rebels with a Catholic queen-in-waiting with a legitimate claim to the throne. This gave purpose to future plots and rebellions, as their outcome would be Mary replacing Elizabeth as queen, as well as the restoration of the Catholic faith. Mary was also able to draw in other conspirators, notably the Duke of Norfolk, who saw that their power and status would be enhanced by marriage to Mary.

Finally, the rebellion demonstrated the possible collusion of foreign powers, notably Spain, which might be prepared to support any rebellion against Elizabeth. It also raised the possibility of collusion between English Catholics and foreign (Catholic) states with the aim of deposing Elizabeth and restoring Catholicism.

2 The defeat of the Northern Revolt strengthened Elizabeth's grip on power because it enabled her to assert her authority in the north of England. About 450 of the rebels were executed, including the Earl of Northumberland. The arrival of the Earl of Huntingdon to lead the Council of the North in 1572 ensured that Catholicism was effectively suppressed. The treason laws were also broadened, making it easier to deal with rebels.

However, the Northern Revolt also weakened Elizabeth's position. The pope excommunicated Elizabeth in 1570 after the revolt had been crushed. This provided an incentive for the rulers of Europe's Catholic nations, including France and Spain, to engage in plots against Elizabeth, including the Ridolfi, Throckmorton and Babington plots. In this sense, Elizabeth's position was weakened rather than strengthened by the revolt. In addition, Mary, Queen of Scots, remained a focal point for future Catholic plots against Elizabeth, as Mary was a queen-in-waiting with a legitimate claim to the throne, and who could depose Elizabeth and restore Catholicism in England. The Northern Revolt, therefore, raised questions about the loyalty of Elizabeth's Catholic subjects, who remained a potential threat to the throne.

16. The Ridolfi plot

The Ridolfi plot was a threat to Elizabeth I because its aims were to murder Elizabeth, launch a Spanish invasion and put Catholic Mary, Queen of Scots, on the throne. The presence of 10 000 Spanish troops in the Netherlands demonstrated that any Catholic plot against Elizabeth could be quickly supported by Spain.

17. The Throckmorton and Babington plots

Both the Throckmorton and Babington plots threatened Elizabeth I because they showed how an alliance of Catholic foreign powers, rebellious Catholics and Mary, Queen of Scots, threatened her hold on the throne. Catholics were now seen as 'the enemy within', as there were 10 000 Spanish troops in the Netherlands as well as a large number of soldiers under the command of the Duke of Guise. Mary, Queen of Scots, continued to conspire with Catholics against Elizabeth, which made her an ongoing threat to the throne. This led to her execution in 1587.

18. Walsingham's spies

Catholic plots were defeated between 1570 and 1586 due to the use of spies. The reluctance of some members of the Catholic nobility and gentry to support these plots and government reprisals deterred further plotting.

Walsingham had an effective network of spies abroad in France, Germany, Spain, Italy and North Africa. He also had paid informants at home in many English towns and in the countryside. He made effective use of ciphers (codes) for all correspondences, while developing the ability to decipher or decode the activities of the plotters. He also made effective use of agents provocateurs. This allowed the plotting to be monitored and unmasked, or plotters arrested, before they became a serious threat to the queen.

Walsingham also made use of repression – 130 Catholic priests and 60 of their supporters were executed. More were tortured. Moreover, the gruesome nature of the executions – for instance, the Babington plotters were hung, drawn and quartered with the gallows being 'mighty high' – sent a powerful message to potential plotters within the Catholic community. This discouraged further plots. Walsingham's methods also meant that many members of the Catholic nobility and gentry, especially in Lancashire, did not back these plots. Many nobles had benefitted from the dissolution of the monasteries under Henry VIII and enjoyed the queen's patronage, and they were not going to risk all this by engaging in conspiracies.

19. The execution of Mary, Queen of Scots

Mary had been involved in a series of plots against Elizabeth, including the revolt of the Northern Earls, the Ridolfi plot, the Throckmorton plot and the Babington plot. This made her an ongoing threat to the queen. Executing Mary would ensure that she would no longer be the focus of plots against Elizabeth.

Walsingham's use of spies, agents provocateurs and ciphers had meant that Elizabeth's government not only knew about Mary's involvement in the Babington plot but also her role within it. This evidence made it easier to convict her of treason, leading to her execution in 1587.

Relations with Spain
20. Spain: political and religious rivalry

1 Two reasons why relations between England and Spain deteriorated between 1566 and 1587 include religious rivalry and revolt in the Netherlands.

Religious rivalry remained important, as Spain was a Catholic country while England now had a Protestant monarch. Philip II of Spain opposed Elizabeth's religious settlement of 1559. This created the fear that Spain would seek to invade England, depose Elizabeth and restore Catholicism, a fear made worse by Spanish involvement in a range of plots and conspiracies, including the Babington plot, the Throckmorton plot and the Ridolfi plot. Spain viewed Protestantism as a dangerous heresy that had to be stamped out.

The revolt in the Netherlands occurred when Dutch Protestants rebelled against Spanish rule. Spain accused England of encouraging the rebels while England worried about the presence of a large Spanish army just across the Channel from England. This situation was made worse by English tolerance of the Sea Beggars – Dutch rebels and sailors who attacked Spanish ships – as well as mercenaries, such as John Casimir. Relations between England and Spain, therefore, declined as England became increasingly involved in resisting Spanish control of the Netherlands, thus angering Spain.

2 Elizabeth's government could be blamed because it had seized the Genoese loan, supported the Dutch rebels and launched attacks on Spanish shipping, which, by the late 1570s, had brought the Spanish Netherlands to the point of bankruptcy. Italian bankers based in Genoa, Italy, made the loan, which was paid in gold, to Philip II's government. The English took the gold from Spanish ships sheltering in English ports on the grounds that it was the property of Italian banks rather than the Spanish government. This action angered Spain, who viewed it as unwarranted interference with Spanish property. Elizabeth's government had damaged relations with Spain through an act of provocation.

Additionally, Elizabeth's government must also take responsibility for declining relations with Spain by encouraging attacks on Spanish shipping in the English Channel and the New World. This involved attacks by Drake on Spanish settlements in the Pacific and Caribbean, as well as attacks by Dutch rebels, the Sea Beggars, on Spanish ships in the English Channel. These actions angered the Spanish and bankrupted the Spanish Netherlands, resulting in the Spanish Fury. From a Spanish point of view, English piracy had done great damage to relations with Spain.

However, Spain was also responsible for declining relations. Spain had taken advantage of the papal bull excommunicating Elizabeth I to involve itself in plots against Elizabeth, notably the Ridolfi plot of 1571. In this sense, relations between Spain and England declined because of the threat Spain posed to England, and not necessarily because of the actions of Elizabeth's government.

21. Spain: commercial rivalry

By the 1560s, England and Spain had emerged as trade rivals. Both wanted the raw materials of the New World as well as trading opportunities in Turkey, Europe, Russia, China and North Africa. This was bound to lead to tensions between the two countries.

The tension was made worse by Spain closing off Antwerp and the Rhine to English traders, especially those involved in the wool trade. This resulted in English support for the Dutch rebels, making relations between the two countries deteriorate further. It also meant that, increasingly, England looked for other trading opportunities, especially in the New World, bringing it into conflict with Spain.

War with Spain
22. The Netherlands and Cadiz

Drake's attack on Cadiz was important because it delayed the construction of the Spanish Armada for a year, giving the English more time to prepare for an attack. It also demonstrated that the English navy could engage at sea with the Spanish, who preferred to board and seize ships, as English cannon could fire more quickly and from further away than their Spanish counterparts. However, the attack was also a provocation to Philip II, encouraging him to construct the Armada as a means of invading England and deposing Elizabeth I.

The Armada
23. Spanish invasion plans

One reason why Philip II launched the Armada was religion: Spain was Catholic, England was Protestant. The pope had excommunicated Elizabeth in 1570. The Armada was a crusade that aimed to return the 'old religion' (Catholicism) to England. Invading England and deposing Elizabeth would enhance the power of the Catholic League and strengthen the Spanish Empire. It would end the threat Elizabeth posed to the Spanish Netherlands.

Another reason was provocation: English privateers had been attacking Spanish ships and colonies in the New World, and Elizabeth's government had been supporting Dutch rebels in the Netherlands. An invasion would be a suitable response to English provocation; it would restore Philip's authority in full.

(Note: you could also mention other reasons including:

- Circumstances seemed to favour the Spanish. Spain had acquired Portugal in 1580. The Duke of Parma had been successful in defeating the Dutch rebels and making them retreat. Elizabeth seemed hesitant to respond to Spain. An invasion now seemed likely to succeed.

- Politics was important because the Treaty of Joinville with France (1584) meant that Spain could attack England without risk of a war with France at the same time. Elizabeth signed the Treaty of Nonsuch (1585) with the Dutch Protestants; this meant that England supported the Dutch rebels, justifying an invasion.)

24. Reasons for the English victory

One reason for the defeat of the Spanish Armada was that English ships were better armed and equipped. In English ships, the cannons were mounted on smaller gun carriages than on Spanish ships. English ships had enough space for cannon to recoil, be quickly reloaded and then pushed back through the gun port. This meant that English ships could fire more cannonballs at the Spanish with more speed, enabling them to seriously damage their ships and undermine the Armada's chances of linking up with the Duke of Parma and invading England.

Another reason was that English tactics were superior. The English sought to get close enough to the Spanish ships to rake them with gunfire but far enough away to prevent them from boarding. This enabled them to severely damage a number of Spanish ships at the battle of Gravelines, in which significant numbers of the Spanish crew were killed. At the same time, Drake's use of fireships caused the Spanish to panic and cut their anchors, drifting out into the North Sea.

(Note: these are not the only reasons you could mention. You could also refer to the weather, the communication problems facing the Spanish, the fact that Spanish ships were poorly supplied, the attack on Cadiz ('The singeing of the King of Spain's beard') and poor Spanish leadership, especially the fact that the commander of the Armada, the Duke of Medina Sidonia, was not an experienced naval officer.)

25. Consequences of the English victory

The defeat of the Spanish Armada did secure Elizabeth's position as queen. It removed the threat of invasion and with it the risk of the queen being deposed. It also seemed to be a major propaganda victory for the queen. Elizabeth, as paintings of the day highlighted, could now be seen as a warrior queen (Gloriana), in this way strengthening her authority among ordinary people as well as the nobility. More importantly, it vindicated Elizabeth's religious settlement, as the victory seemed to demonstrate Divine Providence – God, it seemed, was a Protestant and on the side of Elizabeth and the English. The government was not slow to exploit this, issuing commemorative medals carrying the motif 'God blew and they were scattered.'

However, other things secured Elizabeth's position as queen. The execution of Mary, Queen of Scots, meant that, at a stroke, an alternative Catholic monarch was removed. This denied leadership and purpose to Catholic rebels, making it harder for them to plot against her. In this sense, it is Walsingham's uncovering of the plots against Elizabeth that secured Mary's execution, rather than the defeat of the Spanish Armada, that can be credited with Elizabeth's survival by 1588.

Elizabethan society in the Age of Exploration, 1558–88

Education and leisure
26. Elizabethan education

1 One reason why education changed during Elizabeth I's reign was the growth of trade in the Elizabethan era, as this required ordinary people to be able to read, write and understand mathematics so they could record transactions properly. This gradually encouraged more people to become literate so that they could work effectively.

Another reason was that, by the early 1500s, philosophers, called Humanists, were arguing that education was valuable on its own and not merely a way of preparing people for a role in life. This encouraged more people to either become educated or give educational opportunities to their children.

(Note that there are other points you could make here, including:

- the growth of Protestantism, which encouraged people to read as a way of accessing the Bible

- the printing press, which made books cheaper therefore encouraging reading and education.)

2 Any two of the following features:

- Grammar schools provided an education independently of the Church and charged fees, though scholarships were available.

- The curriculum included the Bible, debating, Latin, French, Greek and philosophy.

- The sons of craftsmen and yeomen farmers were given an education in reading, writing and mathematics that would prepare them for their careers.

27. Sport, pastimes and the theatre

1 Any two of the following ways are valid:
- The lower classes played football, although the rules varied from place to place and the game was exceedingly violent.
- They also participated in and watched wrestling, especially public wrestling matches.
- They attended baiting (with dogs, bears and bulls) and cock-fighting. This often took place in special arenas where money was bet on the outcomes of the fights.

2 The theatre changed in the following ways during Elizabeth's reign:

New literature emerged, including plays by Shakespeare. These were often comedies that contained the vulgar humour enjoyed by many during Elizabeth's reign. The period saw the ending of religious plays, especially the mystery plays popular with Catholics, with many new plays being non-religious or secular.

There was also the development of companies of professional players sponsored by the nobility and even the monarch. These included Leicester's Men, sponsored by Robert Dudley, Earl of Leicester, and the Queen's Men, sponsored by the queen. All actors were male, even those who played women.

Poverty
28. The problem of the poor

Population growth was important in causing poverty in Elizabethan England, as the population grew from 3 million, in 1551, to 4.2 million, by 1601. This increased demand for food, driving up prices while increasing the labour supply and reducing wages.

However, there were other reasons for poverty, including bad harvests, economic recessions – especially caused by trade embargos involving Spain – and enclosure. This drove large numbers of people off the land, as they were unable to provide for their families, creating a population of 'landless labourers' and vagrants.

29. Changing attitudes

One way in which the Elizabethan authorities tried to deal with poverty was to provide assistance to the poor with the aim of helping them improve their position in society. The poor rate, a local tax organised by the Justices of the Peace, raised funds, with the money raised going to improve the lives of the poor. Similarly, charities and the Poor Relief Act of 1576 sought to provide the poor with the means to be able to improve their lives. It was hoped that, by providing assistance to the able bodied poor in this way, the poor would eventually escape poverty.

Another way Elizabethan authorities tried to deal with poverty was to take harsh and repressive measures against the poor, with the aim of deterring vagrancy and begging. The 1572 Vagabonds Act meant that vagrants could be whipped, maimed (a hole was drilled through their ear) or even hanged if caught begging. The authorities viewed the poor, and vagrants in particular, as a threat to property and public order and took harsh measures to deter or discourage vagrancy, so that property could be safeguarded and public order preserved.

Exploration and discovery
30. Factors promoting exploration

One reason why voyages of exploration took place in Elizabethan times was improvements in ship design. The new ships, or galleons, had bigger sails, were faster and more manoeuvrable. They could also concentrate greater firepower, protecting themselves from attacks by pirates, and could also carry more supplies. This meant that ships could undertake longer voyages, leading to exploration of the New World, the Indian Ocean and the Pacific.

(Note that you could explain one of a number of different reasons here, including private investment, trading opportunities and new technology.)

31. Drake's circumnavigation of the globe

One consequence of Drake's circumnavigation of the globe was that England's reputation as a maritime power increased. People increasingly believed that English ships were capable of travelling great distances and could defend themselves from attack. This, in turn, meant that people were prepared to invest in trading expeditions involving English ships, such as those to Virginia under Walter Raleigh in 1580, as well as expeditions to India and the Far East. It also led to the further development of newly discovered trade patterns, such as the triangular trade between England, West Africa and the Caribbean.

Another consequence of Drake's circumnavigation of the globe was Britain's growing naval power. The success of Drake's expedition and the damage inflicted on the Spanish was that Britain not only saw her navy as her primary means of defence, something the defeat of the Spanish Armada demonstrated, but also as a means by which existing and emerging trading interests in the New World, China and India could be defended.

Raleigh and Virginia
32. Raleigh and the attempted colonisation of Virginia

One reason why Raleigh attempted to colonise Virginia was trade. The colonists felt that they could barter ironware, woollen cloth and hunting knives in return for other commodities that could be sold at a profit. They also believed that other valuable items, such as gold and tobacco, could be brought back to England and sold. Raleigh, therefore, saw the colony as an investment where those who provided money (capital) would be able to generate a significant return on the money they had put into it.

(Note: this is only one possible reason. There are others that could be explained. These include:
- The colony, if successful, would lead to other equally successful colonies elsewhere.
- The colony could form a base for privateers to attack Spanish colonies in the New World.
- A successful colony, like the one in Virginia, would make England less dependent on Spain, France and Italy for imported goods.)

33. The failure of Virginia

One reason why the attempt to colonise Virginia failed was because of Indian attack. The colonists, by demanding food from and spreading disease to the local people, do seem to have provoked hostility among the local Indian (Native American) tribes, resulting in Indian attacks led by a local chief, Winginia. These attacks were beaten off but did bring about a crisis that led to the abandonment of the first colony in June 1586. Chief Powhatan may have annihilated the second colony between 1587 and 1590. In both instances, Indian attack led to either the abandonment of the colony (1586) or its destruction (1590).

(Note: this is only one reason among many. You could also explain poor leadership, a lack of food and the war with Spain, which meant that the colony was never properly supplied.)

PRACTICE

41. Practice

5 (a) For each feature, you get one mark for identifying the feature up to a maximum of two features and one mark for adding supporting information.

Feature 1: One feature of the religious settlement was the Act of Supremacy of 1559. This made Elizabeth the Head of the Church of England. All members of the clergy were now required to swear allegiance to her as the Head of the Church.

Feature 2: Another feature was the Act of Uniformity. This introduced a set form of church service in the Book of Common Prayer, to be used in all churches. The clergy had to use the wording of the Prayer Book when conducting services. Anyone who refused to do so was punished.

42. Practice

5 (b) There are 6 marks on offer for AO1 and 6 marks for AO2 in this question. If you do not introduce your own information then you can only get a maximum of 8 marks. Your AO1 information needs to be accurate and relevant and your AO2 needs to provide an explanation of the question.

Attempts to colonise Virginia failed for a number of reasons, including lack of food, Native American (Indian) attack and the war with Spain.

One reason was a lack of food. The colonists arrived in Virginia too late to sow crops while one of their ships, the Tiger, was breached, leading to seawater ruining the food it was carrying. This meant that the colonists failed because they were quickly reduced to near starvation, weakening their health and lowering their morale. This may well have influenced the first colonists' decision to abandon the colony in 1586 and return to England.

This made the settlers increasingly dependent on the Native Americans for food supplies. This meant there had to be regular contact between the settlers and the Algonquian Indians. This encouraged the spread of infectious diseases between the settlers and the Indians, who had no immunity to these infections. The subsequent unexplained deaths of some Native Americans may in turn have provoked attacks on both the first and second colonies by Wingina, and other Native American chiefs who feared that the English had the ability to kill them without touching them. This may have encouraged the first settlers to abandon Roanoke in 1586, and may explain the disappearance of the second colony by 1590.

Linked to this was the war with Spain that had been going on since 1585. This meant that there were few ships left to supply either the first or second colony. This would have left the colonists isolated, denied essential supplies and vulnerable to Native American attack. It is hardly surprising therefore that the first colony was abandoned in 1586 while the second one may have been destroyed by Indian attack.

In conclusion, lack of food appears to have been key to the colonists' failure. This weakened their morale and forced them to deal with the Native Americans with catastrophic results. This was made worse by the war with Spain, which left the colonists isolated.

45. Practice

5 (c) questions have 16 marks on offer: 6 for AO1 and 10 for AO2. Your task is to evaluate the statement and come to a conclusion as to the extent to which you agree with it, justifying your conclusion. This means considering how important the consequence given in the statement is compared to other consequences.

5 (c) (i) Religion was a major issue confronting Elizabeth on her accession to the throne in 1558, as the country was divided between Catholics and Protestants, making a religious settlement difficult. However, Elizabeth also faced other problems: her legitimacy as monarch was in doubt and she faced financial problems, and threats from abroad in the form of Spain and France.

Religion was a major issue confronting Elizabeth. The country was divided between Catholics and Protestants, carrying the prospect of religious wars of the type that were found in France and Germany. Many Catholics would not accept a Protestant monarch on the throne and preferred Catholic alternatives, such as Mary, Queen of Scots. Many bishops appointed by Mary opposed Elizabeth and the religious settlement she tried to impose. Moreover, many Catholic noblemen, including the Nevilles and the Percys, who were powerful within the court and Privy Council under Mary, disliked their isolation under Elizabeth. So, there was always the prospect, especially in the north, of a Catholic revolt against Elizabeth. However, Elizabeth, even as a Protestant monarch, could not ignore the wishes of her more radical Protestant subjects, the Puritans, who demanded an end to vestments and other 'Catholic' symbols and practices. Elizabeth was forced, therefore, into a compromise with her religious settlement, hoping that both the Book of Common Prayer and the Act of Uniformity would satisfy both Catholics and Protestants.

Elizabeth also faced financial problems. The Crown, thanks to Mary's wars with France, was £300 000 in debt and its income had fallen significantly due to the sale of Crown Lands. This made Elizabeth increasingly dependent on parliament for extra taxation, which could result in parliament demanding concessions in return. Moreover, additional taxation would undermine Elizabeth's popularity, making her more vulnerable to rebellion. Alternative strategies, such as debasing the currency by reducing its silver content, would merely result in inflation. Elizabeth, therefore, had to find ways of reducing her debts by managing her expenditure more effectively.

Elizabeth's right to rule, her legitimacy, was also challenged. As the daughter of Anne Boleyn, many argued that she had usurped the throne and that other claimants, including Mary, Queen of Scots, were entitled to rule in her place. Elizabeth was forced, therefore, to constantly demonstrate to her subjects that she was entitled to govern the country.

Finally, Elizabeth also faced problems abroad. France had made peace with England under the Treaty of Cateau-Cambrésis, but, having a bigger population, France posed a threat across the Channel. Mary, Queen of Scots, who had a claim to the throne, was married to Francis II, raising the possibility of a French invasion that would depose Elizabeth and make Mary queen. Finally, the war between France and Spain ended, raising the possibility of the two most powerful Catholic kingdoms in Europe turning against England.

In conclusion, religion was a major problem facing Elizabeth when she became queen in 1558, as it also undermined her legitimacy and made possible both civil war and rebellion. Yet, other problems, such as Elizabeth's financial position and threats from abroad, shaped by the religious differences that existed in Europe, were also important.

49. Practice

5 (c) questions have 16 marks on offer: 6 for AO1 and 10 for AO2. Your task is to evaluate the statement and come to a conclusion as to the extent to which you agree with it, justifying your conclusion. This means considering how important the consequence given in the statement is compared to other consequences.

5 (c) (ii) The Council of the North was a major consequence of the Revolt of the Northern Earls. However, the revolt also brought into focus the potential disloyalty of Catholics, as well as the fact that Mary, Queen of Scots, as an alternative monarch, could encourage further revolts.

The Revolt of the Northern Earls had demonstrated the weakness of Elizabeth's authority in the north of England. The Bishop of Durham had been forced to flee while Catholic masses were widely celebrated in the north of England in defiance of the Act of Uniformity. There was therefore a need to reimpose Elizabeth's authority, which led to the setting up of the Council of the North by 1570. This resulted in the Earl of Huntingdon, a committed Protestant, passing laws that suppressed Catholicism.

However, the Act of Uniformity also brought into focus the potential disloyalty of Catholics. Before the Revolt of the Northern Earls, Catholicism had been quietly tolerated, provided that it did not threaten the Crown. However, the revolt proved otherwise, and, subsequently, Catholics were treated with greater suspicion. This is demonstrated in the number of executions of Catholics carried out – at least 450 – as well as the widening of the definition of treason: it became a treasonable offence to print papal bulls or call the queen a heretic. Pius VI's excommunication of Elizabeth in 1570 further confirmed that Catholics, in the eyes of Elizabeth and her government, could not be trusted.

The Revolt of the Northern Earls also demonstrated the importance of Mary, Queen of Scots, as central to any rebellion against Elizabeth. A key strand in the plot of 1569 was an attempt to marry Mary to the Duke of Norfolk. Moreover, Mary emerges as a key figure in the Ridolfi, Throckmorton and Babington plots against Elizabeth. The Revolt of the Northern Earls, therefore, deepened the existing distrust of Mary that existed in Elizabeth's Court and Privy Council, leading to Mary's execution in 1587.

In conclusion, the Council of the North was an important consequence of the Revolt of the Northern Earls of 1569. However, this was merely a confirmation of the fact that Elizabeth's government could no longer trust Catholics, leading to greater repression of Catholicism in the 1570s and 1580s. Equally importantly, the Revolt of the Northern Earls demonstrated the importance of Mary, Queen of Scots, as a focal point in any rebellions against Elizabeth.

Published by Pearson Education Limited, 80 Strand, London, WC2R 0RL.

www.pearsonschoolsandfecolleges.co.uk

Copies of official specifications for all Pearson qualifications may be found on the website: qualifications.pearson.com

Text and illustrations © Pearson Education Limited 2017

Produced, typeset and illustrated by Tech-Set Ltd, Gateshead

Cover illustration by Eoin Coveney

The right of Brian Dowse to be identified as author of this work has been asserted by him in accordance with the Copyright, Designs and Patents Act 1988.

Content is included from Rob Bircher, Kirsty Taylor, and Victoria Payne.

First published 2017

20 19 18 17

10 9 8 7 6 5 4 3 2

British Library Cataloguing in Publication Data
A catalogue record for this book is available from the British Library

ISBN 978 1 292 16971 2

Printed in Slovakia by Neografia

Acknowledgements
The publisher would like to thank the following for their kind permission to reproduce their photographs:

(Key: b-bottom; c-centre; l-left; r-right; t-top)

Alamy Images: Granger Historical Picture Archive 19, Photo Researchers Inc 23; **Bridgeman Art Library Ltd:** National Portrait Gallery, London, UK 1, National Portrait Gallery, London, UK / Photo © Stefano Baldini 18, Parham House, West Sussex, UK / Photo © Mark Fiennes 22, Private Collection / Photo © Philip Mould Ltd, London 4, Universal History Archive / UIG 10, Woburn Abbey, Bedfordshire, UK 25; **Getty Images:** Hulton Archive 17, Photo12 11

All other images © Pearson Education

Picture Research by: Alison Prior

Notes from the publisher

1.In order to ensure that this resource offers high-quality support for the associated Pearson qualification, it has been through a review process by the awarding body. This process confirms that this resource fully covers the teaching and learning content of the specification or part of a specification at which it is aimed. It also confirms that it demonstrates an appropriate balance between the development of subject skills, knowledge and understanding, in addition to preparation for assessment.

Endorsement does not cover any guidance on assessment activities or processes (e.g. practice questions or advice on how to answer assessment questions), included in the resource nor does it prescribe any particular approach to the teaching or delivery of a related course.

While the publishers have made every attempt to ensure that advice on the qualification and its assessment is accurate, the official specification and associated assessment guidance materials are the only authoritative source of information and should always be referred to for definitive guidance.

Pearson examiners have not contributed to any sections in this resource relevant to examination papers for which they have responsibility.

Examiners will not use endorsed resources as a source of material for any assessment set by Pearson.

Endorsement of a resource does not mean that the resource is required to achieve this Pearson qualification, nor does it mean that it is the only suitable material available to support the qualification, and any resource lists produced by the awarding body shall include this and other appropriate resources.

2.Pearson has robust editorial processes, including answer and fact checks, to ensure the accuracy of the content in this publication, and every effort is made to ensure this publication is free of errors. We are, however, only human, and occasionally errors do occur. Pearson is not liable for any misunderstandings that arise as a result of errors in this publication, but it is our priority to ensure that the content is accurate. If you spot an error, please do contact us at resourcescorrections@pearson.com so we can make sure it is corrected.